THE
ESSENTIAL
Puppy

Consulting Editor
BETSY SIKORA SIINO

Featuring Photographs by
RENÉE STOCKDALE

**HOWELL
BOOK
HOUSE**

Howell Book House

Published by Wiley Publishing, Inc. All rights reserved
Published simultaneously in Canada

For general information about our other products and services, please contact our Customer Care Department within the United States at (800) 762-2974, outside the United States at (317) 572-3993 or fax (317) 572-4002.

Wiley also publishes its books in a variety of electronic formats. Some content that appears in print may not be available in electronic books. For more information about Wiley products, visit our web site at www.wiley.com.

The Essential Puppy is an abridged edition of *The Puppy: An Owner's Guide to a Happy Healthy Pet,* first published in 1996.

Library of Congress Cataloging-in-Publication Data
Library of Congress Cataloging-in-Publication Data
The essential puppy/featuring photographs by Renée Stockdale
   p. cm.
Rev. ed. of Puppy care and training/[Bardi McLennan]. 1996.
Includes bibliographical references and index.
ISBN 0-87605-329-0
1. Puppies   2. Dogs.   I. Stockdale, Renée.   II. McLennan, Bardi.
Puppy care and training.   III. Howell Book House.
SF427.E87   1998   98-3865
636.7'07—dc21   CIP

Manufactured in the United States of America
10 9 8 7 6

Series Directors: Dominique DeVito, Donald Stevens
Series Assistant Director: Jennifer Liberts, Amanda Pisani
Editorial Assistant: Michele Matrisciani
Photography Editor: Sarah Storey
Book Design: Paul Costello
Photography:
   Front cover photo by Close Encounters of the Furry Kind/J. Harrison;
   back cover photo by Mary Bloom
   Courtesy of Diana Robinson: 42, 43, 45, and 46
   All other photos by Renée Stockdale.
Production Team: Stephanie Mohler, Heather Pope, Karen Teo

CHAPTER ONE

Puppy Preparations

Puppies bring with them an abundance of joy—a playful exuberance, a sweet face, and a soft warm body to cuddle. They also arrive in their new homes with an abundance of charm, and they all seem to know exactly how to use it to beguile their new owners. In fact, being taken in by your puppy's charisma may just be what marks the start of a lifelong friendship. The memories of naughtiness fade, but the charm remains.

What you teach, how you teach and when you teach will determine what kind of adult your puppy becomes. If everyone in the household races to answer the phone, one ding-a-ling will be the starter's gun for the puppy, too. On the other hand, you can (and should) teach your puppy to sit-stay when you are on the phone.

Note the use of "teach" rather than "train." Teaching allows your puppy to participate in the learning process. You teach and the pup learns. Training is essentially robotic. Soldiers are trained. Circus animals are trained. Training implies that the pup shouldn't think, but just obey, and

Your new puppy has lots to learn, and needs you to be a fair and consistent teacher.

this methodology should not be used with puppies. Later, if you're considering engaging in competitive obedience with your dog, you may decide to methodically train him. At that point, your puppy will have learned how to understand instructions, and a less flexible training technique would be more appropriate.

The puppy has so much to learn that he may become lax about house rules only because he is in such a hurry to know it all. It is your responsibility (in addition to basic care) to maintain consistency in disciplining the puppy. Discipline in

this case is positive teaching, not punishment. Each person in the family needs to know and to use the same "action" words (sit, come, off, and so on) in the same tone of voice, requiring the same outcome in order not to confuse the puppy. It is truly not complicated—and will be discussed in detail.

PREPARING FOR YOUR PUPPY

There are a few things that you should do before you bring your puppy home. However, if your puppy already resides with you, it's not too late to do them today!

First, you should locate a veterinarian (your pup's second-best friend). You can often get a referral from your pup's breeder, or from friends, relatives or neighbors who take good care of their dogs. Call to make a get-acquainted appointment. In some areas, veterinarians are very busy and can't take on new patients, and you may have to ask for yet another referral. Do not be intimidated. If you do not care for the doctor's manner, personality, office personnel or anything else about the visit, change doctors!

Call your local Canine Control Officer or town official to learn what local laws apply to keeping dogs in your town, and to find out when your puppy will require a license. Ignorance of local ordinances, such as leash laws, can result in stiff fines. A license and tag are usually required for dogs 6 months of age or older. That tag, along with an ID, should be worn on the dog's regular collar (not the training collar) as a means of identification. Tattooing the dog provides a permanent, easily read identification that is recorded by the tattoo registry you select to help locate your dog should

he ever be lost or stolen. The tattoo is usually placed on the inside thigh when the dog is 6 months of age or older so the numbers will be legible when the dog reaches maturity. The site must then be kept free of hair. The new microchip implant form of identification also has its supporters, but to read the "chip" you need a special device that may not be readily available in your area.

A license and tag are usually required by law for a dog over the age of 6 months.

PUPPY ESSENTIALS

Your new puppy will need:

food bowl	bed
water bowl	crate
collar	toys
leash	grooming supplies
ID tag	

If you haven't found a suitable veterinarian and made sure that your puppy is easily identified, put these activities at the top of your "must do" list for tomorrow.

YOUR NEW PUPPY NEEDS *YOU*

What your new puppy needs most is *you*—a responsible person to be at home while he is learning what he can and can't do. If no one is home to take on this job, the pup must teach himself. Puppies are quick to learn, and that is exactly how puppy problems begin. Left to make his own decisions, his idea of what he can do is not governed by whether you consider it good or bad.

A puppy looks at life from his own unique perspective: If he is able

to do it, it must be okay. So he will engage in pulling down the curtains, chewing the rug, spreading the trash all over the floor and so on as soon as he discovers he is indeed able and no one is around to prevent his mistakes. Puppies should not be punished for these "normal" (though unacceptable) behaviors, because it is the owner who is at fault for not preventing them.

So let's hope you chose a good time to bring the new puppy home—when whoever is in charge of teaching the pup his first lessons in acceptable family manners is home most of the day. The beginning of a vacation period is a good choice for those who work.

FOOD AND WATER BOWLS

Apart from a responsible human being, the puppy needs a variety of basic items. Topping the list are a food dish and a separate water bowl. A waterproof mat to put them on is not just for decoration—it will save the floor from slurped water and spilled food. If your pup has long, hanging ears, get dishes specially made to keep such ears out of the food or water. (This also saves on cleaning ears twenty times a day and mopping the kitchen when he shakes.) Consider bowls with weighted bases or nonslip bottoms so the pup can't push them all around the room. For a dog that will be very tall, two dishes in a raised stand will keep food and water where they belong and at a comfortable height.

FOOD

Begin feeding your puppy with whatever dog food he was fed by the breeder. If you can't find out, ask your veterinarian for a recommendation, or buy a top-quality food made especially for puppies.

Don't forget the cookies! Small, plain dog biscuits are fine for "Good puppy!" rewards and an occasional treat. Fancy flavored treats are okay for adult dogs, but young puppies do better on a blander diet—and fewer treats! (Detailed information on feeding appears in chapter 2.)

COLLAR AND LEASH

It is very sad to see a little puppy weighed down with a heavy chain collar and a leash strong enough to restrain a cow! Be sure each collar and leash you select matches the current size and strength of your puppy. Take your pup with you to the pet store to be sure that you get the right collar, and just keep in mind that you'll probably be back in a few months for a bigger one! The leash should last longer. Unless, of course, your puppy is allowed to use it as a teething toy—definitely not a recommended game.

You can put an ID tag on your pup's collar, but he probably won't need a license tag until 6 months of age (check with your local officials), at which time you will also add a rabies tag. That's a lot of hardware

Your puppy will need several different collars and leashes as he grows, so start out small.

5

for a small-sized puppy! *Warning:* A training (or "choke") collar should not be used on young, developing puppies, and should never be left on a dog—especially not on a puppy. Stay with soft buckle or snap-closure collars for everyday wear. If you choose to train using "motivational" methods only, you'll be staying with the soft collar.

CRATE AND/OR BED

Dogs are animals that have natural denning instincts, and usually take to sleeping in their crates with little resistance.

Your puppy needs a crate. It is a puppy's "bed of choice," a private, personal, snug den where he can sleep, chew a toy and watch the world around him, completely undisturbed. (This is such an important aspect of your puppy's life that much of chapter 4 is devoted to information on the use of a crate.) Crates come in two styles: closed (fiberglass) or open (wire). Each type has an advantage and a disadvantage. The closed crate is draft-proof, but some pups (and their owners) feel that they prevent the dog from fully seeing and engaging in his environment. The open variety offers greater visibility, but most dogs like the crate covered at bedtime. Either type must be placed away from drafts and sources of heat, direct sunlight or air-conditioning.

Regardless of which style you decide on, it's important to get the correct size. This is not a puppy playroom or a canine condo. It is basically a bed and the pup will curl up in about one-third of the space. Gauge the adult size of your pup and get a crate that will just allow him to stand, turn around and lie down. If that size gives him more space than he needs for the next few months, use an adjustable barrier that can be moved back as needed.

The best puppy bedding is a folded bath towel. It's washable or disposable—accidents happen in the best of homes!

Make sure to have a few toys among the supplies you purchase before bringing your new puppy home.

KEEPING PUPPY CONFINED

You will need something called an exercise-pen ("ex-pen"; read: playpen) if your puppy can't be confined to the kitchen or other safe area by means of doors or gates. The exercise-pen will keep your puppy safe, but it also provides room to play, have access to water and use newspapers for a bathroom break if he's a latchkey pet with no one home during the day to take him outside.

The "gate" mentioned is the good old-fashioned baby gate, now sold in pet stores as a "pet gate." Choose one that fits your doorway securely, is high enough that the pup can't easily jump over it and is constructed so that the pup won't be encouraged to try his climbing techniques.

GROOMING TOOLS

Your new puppy needs to be groomed at least once or twice a

HOUSEHOLD DANGERS

Curious puppies and inquisitive dogs get into trouble not because they are bad, but simply because they want to investigate the world around them. It's our job to protect our dogs from harmful substances, like the following:

In the House

cleaners, especially pine oil

perfumes, colognes, aftershaves

medications, vitamins

office and craft supplies

electric cords

chicken or turkey bones

chocolate

some house and garden plants, like ivy,
    oleander and poinsettia

In the Garage

antifreeze

garden supplies, like snail and slug bait,
    pesticides, fertilizers, mouse and rat
    poisons

week. Even the Mexican Hairless needs special attention (sunblock, for one thing!). There are special brushes and combs for every type of coat. Most puppies will shed their puppy coat as the adult coat grows in. This shedding causes mats in longhaired

dogs—and results in speckled furniture and clothing from shorthaired dogs. Your puppy definitely needs a brush! He will also need his nails clipped. (How to clip your puppy's nails is discussed in chapter 3.)

TOYS

Last, but not least, you will need an assortment of appropriate toys—appropriate for your puppy's size, age and personal preferences. Safe, fun and interactive doggy toys abound. If your new puppy is your "only child," you'll be tempted to buy one of each. So when you come home with a shopping bag full, give the puppy one or two, possibly add a third later and save the rest for another day. The old adage that "variety is the spice of life" applies to dog toys. Every few days, add a new toy and subtract an oldie, always letting the favorite toy remain as puppy's security blanket.

One good interactive toy is the red, hard rubber "beehive" toy that bounces erratically when dropped. (The pup will soon learn to drop it himself.) Some balls are meant to be thrown and retrieved; others like the big Boomer ball can be pushed, hit and nosed by the pup alone. A ball with a bell inside maintains the pup's interest in the game. Rope toys are great for solitary chewing. Rawhides also offer hours of chewing, and so serve a more occupational purpose than just play. Plush dinosaurs, spiny hedgehogs, fleece-stuffed toys and numerous other characters that produce sounds that range from squeaks to roars abound. Have fun!

Watch your puppy when he's playing with chew toys, because not every toy is safe for every dog. Some dogs confuse the concept of "play" with "destroy" and are interested only in terminating or swallowing whatever you buy. Stick with toys that require your participation, or, for solitary play, give your puppy the larger-sized hard rubber toys and balls and good-sized rawhide bones.

PUPPY-PROOF YOUR HOME

Making your home safe for the new puppy will require you to make the same careful preparations as needed for a toddler. The puppy must learn that some items and some areas are off limits. Teach by prevention! Use a guttural "accht!" instead of "no." It

will sound more like the warning growl from the pup's mother.

PUT HAZARDS OUT OF REACH

Begin by taking the obvious precautions. Put all solvents, chemicals, medications and the like out of reach. This means that anything that could be considered potentially harmful must be stored higher than the full-grown dog can jump, or behind cupboard doors that cannot be pried open. Paws and noses are incredibly adept at opening almost anything that's closed! The plastic catches sold to keep toddlers out of

Puppies are often insatiably curious, so you must be diligent in keeping household dangers out of their reach.

9

During those times when you can't keep an eye on your puppy, confine him, either to his crate or to a small area of the house, with the use of a baby gate.

kitchen cabinets and other storage places work well for keeping dogs out, too.

Now is the time to read product labels. If there's a poison warning on the container, be sure everyone in the household knows it and place the item on a high shelf in the garage or another safe place. Prescription medicines *and* all over-the-counter medications should be kept behind closed doors. You probably don't consider things you use every day for personal hygiene as dangerous, but mouthwash, toothpaste, soap, deodorants and the like are poison to puppies. Be sure to discard the empty containers where the dog can't get at them.

Granted, you can't hide everything you own, or live in an empty shell, but you can take steps to avoid disaster. First, *be aware* of both dangers and of what your pup is doing. Second, *confine* your puppy whenever you can't keep an eye on him. In other words, use the crate and use pet gates. Putting dangerous items out of reach is merely a simple way to make your job of teaching easier. If all these things are lying around, you'll be saying, "accht!" all day long—and what little puppy wants to hear that? By puppy-proofing your house, you've removed the dangers and can proceed with positive training. Your new pet will get smiles and praise and learn quickly what he needs to do to earn them. The occasional, necessary "accht" will then have powerful meaning.

INDOORS AND OUTDOORS

Protect your puppy from every outside door that does not lead to a safely fenced-in yard. All it takes is for the door to be opened a crack, and the pup can slip through to become another lost-dog statistic. Outside, check gates—constantly!

As a protection for muscles, joints and bones, keep the puppy on flooring where he has traction. Slippery floors can cause all kinds of damage to growing pups.

POISONOUS PLANTS

Attractive, innocent-looking plants that you've probably nursed along for years may be poisonous to dogs, particularly puppies that are in the business of utilizing all their senses, including taste.

Some of the common houseplants that are poisonous include ivy, Dieffenbachia (or dumbcane), poinsettia, Jerusalem cherry and philodendron. Once you get outdoors, the list goes on and on, from all bulbs (not necessarily the plant, just the bulb and root system) like daffodils and tulips, to many flowering shrubs and trees.

Among the common garden plants that are especially harmful to puppies (and can be fatal) are foxglove, chrysanthemum leaves, larkspur, ivy, yew, ilex, holly, hydrangea, azalea and many of the wild berry-bearing plants such as elderberry and chokecherry. Mushrooms of every kind, including toadstools, can be fatal.

POISONING EMERGENCIES

If you believe that your dog has ingested a poisonous plant or other toxic substance, such as a pesticide or antifreeze, take action! Call the National Animal Poison Control Center (NAPCC) at 1-800-548-2423 or 1-900-680-0000 immediately. You will be charged for the call.

This warning is not meant to terrify you, but only to inform you so you'll take another look at your garden (indoors and out). As an added precaution against any plants you are not sure about, or ones that you value and don't want chewed or dug up, several garden repellent products are on the market. Check to be sure that they are safe for puppies.

If you suspect that your puppy has been sickened by something he's ingested, try to determine what he ate, and call the animal poison control center.

11

OTHER SMALL CREATURES

If you have small animals, such as hamsters, in your home, several precautions are in order. However, the most important precaution is simple: *separation*. No matter how sweet, dear and adorable your little puppy may be, he is first and foremost a dog. Dogs rarely tolerate little creatures like mice, gerbils and hamsters. Chase is the name of the game, and "catch" is the sad end of it.

Be certain that children understand that their other pets must never (*never*) be out of their cages if the puppy is in the room or can push his way into the room. Despite magazine pictures that you see to the contrary, the species do not instinctively mix socially. (Those photos are carefully posed with highly trained animals by exceptional trainers!)

While houseplants and flowers are beautiful accents to your living space, they can be dangerous to a curious young puppy.

CATS

Cats and kittens can be carefully introduced to dogs (preferably older cats to puppies, kittens to adult dogs) and even after a rocky start, most will settle down. They will either become bosom buddies, or a love-hate relationship will keep them forever at a safe distance. Their owners learn to live with it.

Introduce the two by leaving the pup in his crate to allow the cat time to investigate. When the hissing and/or barking desist, hold the puppy in your lap and let the cat proceed with feline caution. Do not hold the kitty or you could be scratched to pieces! Be careful, too, that the pup doesn't get scratched around the eyes or face. (Wash the area immediately and thoroughly if this happens.)

Generally the cat will run off (or more accurately, run up) to where it feels safe, leaving the puppy deprived of the chase. This is fine. The puppy has learned that cats play by different rules than dogs.

12

Cats and dogs can be relied upon to live with one another as good buddies, if they're introduced to each other when young.

VALUABLES

Puppies have no idea of material values, and it's strange how few people realize this until it's too late. Put your precious china ornaments up high (or away) if a long tail will wipe them off the coffee table. Remove the Persian rug from the hallway and store it away until your puppy is old enough to be thoroughly housetrained. Make sure that electrical wires are too high for your puppy to chew or pull at. Fold back ends of runners or tablecloths that hang over the table edge ready to be yanked in the blink of an eye.

Treat your new puppy like a toddler and be thankful that he will learn acceptable behavior in a matter of months, or almost as quickly as you can teach him. A puppy goes from toddler to teen to adult in about two years.

CHAPTER TWO

Food and Fun

Other than you, there is not much your puppy wants more than his food. And because you are the source of food, you score twice. You need to know how a puppy views food, because fussy or problem eaters are generally *made,* not *born.* Rapidly growing puppies have an intense desire as well as the obvious need to be fed—a puppy has to eat in order to grow. But the "desire" is a surefire way for the puppy to go after attention, and that's where your teaching comes in. If you fall for all the puppy's cute, darling and adorable ways of begging for food, you will have a nuisance-beggar for years to come.

Hence, correctly used, food is a ready-made teaching tool, and you can use it to teach a lot more than table manners. Feeding your puppy goes well beyond putting a bowl of dog food on the floor. Ask for something in return—a sit, a paw, a say "please" or whatever—but let the puppy know that food comes with a price.

WHERE TO FEED

Pick a place in the kitchen to feed your puppy that is low in traffic, then stick to that one spot. The water bowl stays there. The food dish is put down and removed after fifteen to twenty minutes. Dogs like to know exactly where and when meals will be served day after day.

WHEN TO FEED

For the first few days, stay with whatever feeding schedule your puppy has been on so you don't upset his internal clock.

Feed a puppy that is 8 to 12 weeks old four times a day. Avoid feeding late at night by working on a schedule of 7 a.m., 11 a.m. (or noon), 3 p.m. and 6 p.m. At about 12 weeks, eliminate the afternoon

meal and for small to medium breeds, reduce feedings to two meals a day at 6 months. Large breeds can remain on three meals a day until 12 or even 18 months. Smaller, more frequent meals help to diminish the likelihood of developing bloat—to which large breeds are particularly susceptible. Two feedings a day will help keep an adult dog healthy and satisfied.

WHAT TO FEED

You are feeding a rapidly growing puppy not to satisfy his appetite, but to make him as healthy an adult dog as possible. The extra you pay for a

Pick a quiet, low-traffic part of the kitchen as the spot in which to feed your puppy.

HOW TO READ THE DOG FOOD LABEL

With so many choices on the market, how can you be sure that you are feeding the right food for your dog? The information is all there on the label—if you know what you're looking for.

Look for the nutritional claims right up top. The package should state that the food is "100% nutritionally complete." Furthermore, it should state its life stage purpose, such as "all life stages." "Growth and maintenance," on the other hand, is for early development, and puppy foods are marked as such. Foods for senior dogs are labelled accordingly.

Ingredients are listed in descending order by weight. The first three or four ingredients will tell you the bulk of what the food contains. Look for the highest-quality ingredients, like meats and grains, to be among them.

The guaranteed analysis tells you what levels of protein, fat, fiber and moisture are in the food, in that order. While these numbers are meaningful, they won't tell you much about the quality of the food. Nutritional value is in the dry matter, not the moisture content.

In many ways, seeing is believing. If your dog has bright eyes, a shiny coat, a good appetite and a good energy level, chances are that his diet is fine. Your dog's breeder and your veterinarian are good sources of advice if you're still confused.

premium puppy food could end up saving you large sums of money in later health-care costs.

Small to medium breeds are fed a growth (or puppy) food three times a day until they are about 6 months of age, when you can cut back to feeding twice a day. Usually, a puppy will begin to leave some or most of the midday meal as an indication that it is no longer needed. When a pup has reached 90 percent of his full height (between 9 and 12 months of age), it's time to switch to a maintenance diet that provides fewer calories.

Large breeds, such as German Shepherd Dogs and Golden or Labrador Retrievers, can be switched over to a maintenance diet sooner. Doing so will help to slow down their rate of growth, as they take longer to mature (twelve to twenty-four months).

Which Food Is Best?

Keep your puppy on the same food that he has been eating unless it is not a top commercial-brand dog food especially formulated for puppies, your veterinarian advises a different food or your puppy is not thriving (check with the veterinarian first). Then, and only then, is a change in order.

Your puppy's veterinarian will recommend a quality puppy food if you are confused by the array on the store shelves. Make the switch gradually over a period of three or four days to avoid stress or stomach upsets, and do it by substituting—not adding! Replace a small amount of the original food with the new. Increase the amount of new food each day, as you decrease the unwanted food, until the change is complete.

Many breeders and canine nutritionists today agree that what's best for the dog—and what the dog likes best—is a combination of one-quarter canned meat mixed with three-quarters kibble (or dry) dog food. The meat is good for them and adds the taste and scent dogs enjoy, which encourages sluggish eaters. Most healthy puppies, however, tend to "inhale" their food, and the kibble slows them down, gives them chewing exercise and helps to reduce tartar accumulation on the molars (crushing teeth). But for an 8-to-12-week-old puppy of a small breed, you can soak the kibble in warm water to soften it for tiny teeth, changing to a dry serving as permanent teeth erupt.

Quality puppy or "growth" commercial formulas contain all the vitamins and minerals required by growing pups of all breeds or sizes. Semi-moist foods might be handy for camping trips with an adult dog, but are not recommended for puppies because they are high in caloric content and artificial colorings, and can cause tartar buildup.

How Much to Feed

The feeding instructions on bags and cans of commercial dog foods are often too generous. Be guided by the fact that a young puppy will

Feed your puppy on a regular schedule.

17

consume what his stomach can comfortably hold in about fifteen to twenty minutes, after which the dish should be removed. Do not leave it longer than that. This is the source (you) at work, establishing good eating habits!

Your puppy's appearance will also provide a good guide for how much to feed. His coat should be glossy, his eyes bright and clear, his teeth coming in straight and free of tartar. You should be able to feel his ribs. A puppy that is too round and roly-poly is unhealthy. The puppy could have internal parasites or just too many calories. Fresh, clean water is every bit as important as food and should be available at all times.

A shiny coat and bright eyes are the best indicators that your puppy's diet is adequate and well-balanced.

But puppies, like people, are individuals, eating habits included— just be sure you're not being conned! Most puppies are convinced they are starving. Those pathetic whines and soulful eyes pleading for seconds (or dessert) could be masking a full stomach! Obesity is the number one nutritional disorder in dogs of all ages. A puppy does not need diet food, but he does need diet management. Be sure that children understand that puppies do not get pieces of jelly doughnuts, hamburger rolls, French fries or other goodies under the table. Speaking of kids and goodies, remind everyone that chocolate is poisonous to dogs.

FEEDING CONCERNS

What if your puppy stops eating? A puppy that doesn't eat any food at all for twenty-four hours should be taken to the veterinarian. No healthy puppy that is offered food three or four times a day (and has it removed after fifteen minutes) ever starved. Dogs are manipulative, but not stupid! Conversely, a dog that eats well but appears to be genuinely hungry all day in between meals should be checked by your veterinarian.

Treats

Treats equate with love: They are just as pleasurable to give as to receive. Just be sure you (and everyone else in the household) realize that treats are food. They should be doled out in tiny portions. If you reward your puppy with a treat and he lies down to chew it, it was probably too large. Consider it part of his dinner. A true treat is a reward that's small enough to be swallowed after one crunch. It's a taste. Just say "No" to bones. Bones were given to dogs in the past because they satisfied the dog's need to chew and gnaw, and a bone from the butcher (or the dinner table) was the only item available. This was also before people worried about the dangers of splintered bones stuck in the throat or intestinal tract, risking a dog's health and requiring costly trips to the vet. And long before anyone even thought about making toys especially for pets!

Dog Food Do's and Don'ts

Do keep small children away from the puppy while he's eating. A puppy is in the process of being

TYPES OF FOOD AND TREATS

There are three types of commercially available dog food—dry, canned and semi-moist—and a huge assortment of treats (lucky dogs!) to feed your dog. Which should you choose?

Dry and canned foods contain similar ingredients. The primary difference between them is their moisture content. The moisture is not just water. It's blood and broth, too, the very things that dogs adore. So while canned food is more palatable, dry food is more economical, convenient and effective in controlling tartar buildup. Many owners feed a 25% canned/75% dry diet to give their dogs the benefit of both types of food. Just be sure your dog is getting the nutrition he needs (you and your veterinarian can make this determination).

Semi-moist foods have the flavor dogs love and the convenience owners want. However, they tend to contain excessive amounts of artificial colors and preservatives.

Dog treats come in every size, shape and flavor imaginable, from organic cookies shaped like postmen to beefy chew sticks. Most dogs seem to love them all, so enjoy the variety. Just be sure not to overindulge your dog. Factor treats into your puppy's regular daily meal sizes.

taught that he does not have to guard food and little children are perceived as a threat because they

that includes keeping a hands-off safe distance once the dog is eating.

From the beginning, show your pup that you are the source of food and you are to be respected! Get him to watch you take out a few kibbles before you put his dish on the floor. Then let him eat them, as a treat, out of your hand—gently. If he nips or snatches, close your hand and stand up. Use the word "gentle" as he's licking your fingers. Then tell him "Good dog!"

When he has learned to sit on command, he can be asked to sit before you put the dish down. Keeping your hand beside the dish for a moment establishes trust. If there's one growl or snarl, the dish is removed and the puppy is put back on a sit. Release him, wait a few minutes and repeat the whole process. He's a smart puppy. He'll quickly catch on to your lesson in table manners!

In everything you do with and for your puppy, remember that you are teaching him. You are teaching him what you want him to do, how to do it and that he can trust the people in his new family. Food is a major lesson in trust. A dog can't fix his own meals, so he must trust you to do it, which is why consistency is

Understand that dogs are very territorial about food, and make sure that your children know how to feed the dog without making him feel threatened.

are so close to the dish! Puppies often consider young children as littermates and therefore competitors, especially for food. Play it safe. A puppy (or adult dog) may accept the child squatting down to watch him eat today, only to retaliate tomorrow.

Children are bitten because they do not understand the importance of food to an animal, and because neither the children nor the pup have been taught how to interact where food is involved. An older child of 7 or 8 will want to feed the puppy himself, but he still needs to be taught exactly how to do it, and so important. Same times, same place, same food.

Remember, fresh, clean water must be available until bedtime. That is just as important as food.

EXERCISE

Sufficient exercise is very important to your puppy's growth (and pleasure). Puppy workouts take many forms, some solo, some with members of his new family. Play, eat and sleep are what puppies do best. (Okay. Add piddle and poop.) A puppy can play alone, but the games puppies shared with their littermates were more fun, and now the new members of the family take on the role of playmates.

Jogging and running are not the right kind of exercise for a puppy, not even a big puppy. In fact, the larger the dog will be, the more you need to limit his physical exercise (including jogging, running and jumping) until maturity. Have your veterinarian check the dog for soundness (heart, hips and the like) at 12 to 18 months. Dogs will always try to keep up with you, to perform whatever you ask them to do, so it is up to you to set the limits. Leaping over hurdles, 2-mile

trots and flying Frisbee catches are for full-grown, physically sound adults, not puppies.

Puppies get most of their exercise from energetic play with four feet on the ground. Chase is a favorite game because it is instinctive, so whether the "prey" is a large and indestructible Boomer ball for a Rottie puppy or a small squeaky ball rolled on the floor for a Yorkie, the game is the same.

Walking the Dog

There are different kinds of walks. One is the "bathroom break" or "business trip," which really isn't a walk at all. The puppy is on lead and is taken to the place where he's meant to relieve himself.

Another kind of walk is the training variety. Puppy is on lead and bouncing around while you try to get him to follow you. Eventually he does and with lots of practice, you'll both graduate to the next two kinds of walks.

The "exercise walk" is, in large measure, for the benefit of the owner. The person is getting his or her muscle tone up and excess fat down, and it is a very intense, no-nonsense, nonstop regimen. Dogs go

22

Exercise is an important aspect of your dog's daily routine.

along because they don't have a choice. This walk is strictly for adult dogs. Puppies need not apply. In fact, all exercise should be curtailed in warm weather and even eliminated (or at least relegated to the evening or early morning) when it gets hot. Heatstroke is dangerous at best, fatal at worst. Prevention is the best cure.

But then there is the "dog's walk," the one where the puppy gets to sniff everything along the way, and to stop to greet other dogs and people. It is pure pleasure, the stuff canine heaven must be made of, and what's more, it is also very good for you, the owner. It is a calming form of exercise and allows you to teach-as-you-go. The puppy learns to greet other dogs nicely, not jump up when you greet friends, to sit or stand quietly when patted and admired.

For now, this walk comes under the heading of "socializing your puppy," but this is the truly companionable walk that begins in puppyhood and is never outgrown.

CHAPTER THREE

Pretty Puppy

Maybe you think you can skip this section because you have a smooth-coated puppy that you've been told doesn't need to be groomed. Wrong! All dogs must be groomed. As a bonus, your puppy will learn that it's okay to have someone run his or her hands over every inch of her body, and there will be no trauma or stress when being examined by the veterinarian, worked on by a professional groomer or a trainer or perhaps eventually given the once-over by a conformation show judge. Besides, dogs think they are very special when they've had grooming attention.

WHERE TO GROOM

Begin grooming with the puppy off the ground, at about the level of your waist. If you try to groom a dog on the ground, she has the advantage—you're on her turf and she's faster on four feet than you are! Get her up off the floor and you will be in control. If you don't have a grooming table, use any sturdy table, workbench or countertop. Add a mat (a car floor mat or a thin rubber doormat are both good choices) so the pup will feel secure and won't slip.

In a pet-supply store you can get a grooming arm that clamps onto any tabletop and that, with a noose, will help keep the dog in place. There is always the danger of a puppy (or an adult dog) stepping off the edge of the grooming area, so get in the habit of keeping one hand (and both eyes) on the pup at all times, especially if you use a grooming noose.

A very tiny puppy—especially one with a long coat—may be brushed for the first few times while lying in your lap. This will help make the pup comfortable while you practice using the brush and comb. Grooming dogs (even puppies) with long coats does take time, so these puppies have to be taught to lie

quietly on either side while you work. It's a struggle at first, but soon the dog will use the time to catch a nap. Keep the first grooming sessions very short—a maximum of ten minutes.

GROOMING TOOLS

You also need the right tools for the job. For a smooth-coated pup, you need a soft bristle brush, a sisal mitt or a rubber curry brush to stimulate the skin to keep it healthy and to distribute the natural oils in the coat. A good comb for a short-haired puppy is a double-toothed flea comb (one side has finer teeth than the other). It will pull out any foreign objects like ticks, fleas or burrs.

For a puppy with a thick, long or wire coat, you will need a metal comb and a brush made for your puppy's type of coat. A groomer or pet-store staff will help you choose the right tools. Pet-supply catalogs also list pages of these grooming tools, many of which are designed specifically for certain breeds. If you decide on a "slicker" (or bent-wire) brush, get the "soft" type for a puppy. Use it gently and only through the hair because the wire will scratch the skin if you brush too hard.

There are several types of tools made to break up mats, as well as special shedding tools for both long- and short-haired dogs.

TRIMMING NAILS

Nails need to be trimmed regularly, and there are two basic types of trimmers to consider. One type works like a regular scissors, and the other slices the nail guillotine-fashion when the two spring-operated handles are squeezed. Special nail trimmers are made for small dogs (or puppies) and others are made for big dogs whose large nails require a strong implement to do the job.

Only the tip that grows out beyond the quick is cut. On white nails, the quick is easier to see than on black nails. Your veterinarian or groomer can show you how to cut your puppy's nails, or you can make regular trips to the groomer's for nail trimming. Overgrown nails can cause a variety of problems from painful walking to deformities requiring surgery.

BRUSHING

Brushing is done from the skin out to the ends of the hairs, slowly and

Training your dog to accept having her nails trimmed when she is a young puppy will make this part of the grooming routine easier when she is a full-grown adult.

25

methodically on long-haired dogs. A mistake most people make is only to brush the ends or the top surface so mats form close to the skin, and in no time the pretty puppy has to be shaved. Regular weekly brushing is a must, and for some longhaired breeds (Yorkshire Terriers are just one example), a quick daily brush-out is even better. If mats are getting even slightly ahead of you, phone the groomer.

EAR CARE

Using a clean, dampened cloth, wipe the inside flap of the puppy's ears. The inside of the ear has a natural light coating of wax that should not

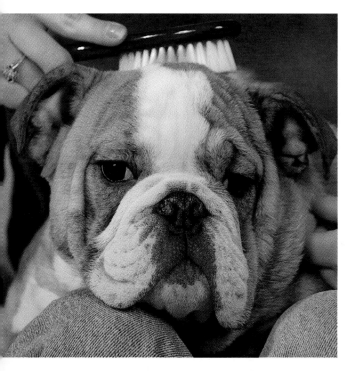

A weekly brushing will keep your puppy's coat healthy and help reduce shedding.

wipe away any accumulation of debris, but take the opportunity to check for mucous discharge, healthy eyelids and clear, healthy-looking eyes.

BATHING

You may shampoo a young puppy, but it's better not to unless there is a valid reason, such as a bad case of fleas. However, it is hard to resist giving a little ball of fluff a beauty treatment. First, thoroughly brush out the dog's coat. Mats will be impossible to untangle later. Put a cotton ball in each ear to keep the water out, and a drop of mineral oil in each eye.

Work in a warm room. Use quite warm water (the pup's body temperature is higher than yours) and only use shampoo or flea products made specifically for puppies. Put a towel in the sink or tub for safe footing, and use a spray attachment to help get out every bit of soap. You cannot rinse too much. Towel dry and/or blow dry with a hair dryer set on warm, not hot, and held at least 18 inches or more away from the dog. Brush the coat carefully as it dries to avoid snarls and that enemy of long hair, mats.

be removed. If the ear is really dirty (a long walk on a dusty road might do it), dampen a piece of gauze or cotton in mineral oil and gently wipe out the dirt. Be careful not to push dirt further into the ear. If there is a foul odor or excessive wax, consult your veterinarian. Never go into the ear with a cotton swab—ever!

EYE CARE

Clean around the eyes using a cotton ball dampened in clean warm water—one for each eye. Gently

CHAPTER FOUR

Housetraining

Housetraining is sometimes called housebreaking. It's easy to see how that word gets confused with all kinds of other things puppies do, none of which are what any owner of a new puppy has in mind! So "housetraining" it is, and it begins the minute you walk in the door with your new puppy. (It is almost impossible to housetrain a puppy that is infested with worms, so a speedy vet-check for worms is a must.)

ESTABLISHING RULES

Each and every person who is involved in housetraining the puppy needs to understand the rules.

As soon as you arrive home with the puppy, take him out on a leash to the small area where you want him to eliminate. This can be behind a bush in the garden, on crushed stone in a dog run or beside

Make sure you praise your dog as he eliminates, so that he understands what you're praising him for.

the curb in the city. It is essential to keep the pup on leash!

You are not taking the puppy for a walk. Walks come later. Consider this a "business trip." Take him to his spot (of your choosing) and stand there. No chit-chat. Pretend not even to look at him. Occasionally a pup will decide to sit while you stand (they know more about obedience than you think!). If this happens, just take a few steps this way and that to get the puppy moving about. This part takes time, but it's time well spent.

Stay beside the puppy so you can say "Good dog!" as he eliminates. Food rewards are inappropriate. All the puppy needs is your approval.

The timing of everything you say or do to a puppy—whether it is praise, a preventive warning or a correction—must be done as that specific action occurs. Praising the pup after he has relieved himself only tells him that you approve of the way he is now walking. Obviously, that's not what you meant!

Dogs like to have one designated area in which to relieve themselves. It's up to you to keep the area clean and attractive to the dog. Once the pup catches on to eliminating there, you can add a command word if you like. Say "Go potty" (or whatever simple phrase you wish) as you reach the spot. You'll get plenty of practice—at 8 to 10 weeks of age, pups need to eliminate about every two hours.

After the pup has relieved himself take a few minutes to play outdoors, or back inside. When the puppy is older, this will be a good time for a walk.

USING A CRATE

When a new puppy comes to your home, it's prime time for using a crate. This essential piece of canine equipment is described in chapter 1. Housetraining begins with the crate.

Call it a crate or a bed or a den, but not a "cage" (that's a four-letter word); it is your pup's home at home or away, his refuge in times of stress (yours or his) and an ideal spot for an undisturbed nap. It is an invaluable tool for housetraining.

Puppies instinctively want to keep their dens clean, so all you have to do is to provide the "den" (crate) and stick to a schedule that allows your puppy to maintain that goal of cleanliness. Your new puppy may have learned all about a crate before he arrived at your home and need nothing more than to know where you keep it. Lucky you! For the rest of the new puppy owners, here's the procedure.

Don't worry if the puppy is more cautious than curious at first. He's being sensible about something that might be dangerous! Do not push, shove or in any way try to force him into the crate. The situation calls for the art of gentle persuasion. Sweet-talk him into overcoming his doubts by interesting him in a toy and then tossing it into the crate. Or let him see and sniff a small treat in your hand as your hand goes into the crate. (Where a yummy treat goes, a pup is sure to follow.) As one paw steps inside, add the now-familiar "Good dog—good crate!"

29

Keep your puppy on a regular schedule so that you can use to your advantage his natural instincts not to eliminate in his "den."

SOME DO'S AND DON'TS

Don't return to the room if the crated pup is fussing.

Don't let him out of the crate while he's complaining.

Do let him eliminate first if he will be crated for an hour or more.

Don't blame the puppy for accidents you could have prevented.

Don't use the crate for punishment.

Do remind children that the dog's crate is off-limits.

Don't feed the puppy in the crate.

Don't let your puppy think his name is "NO!"

Don't nag.

Slowly but Surely

Leave the door open for now, and if he does an instant turnaround (or backs out unceremoniously), that's normal. Make no comment, because the puppy is never praised for coming out, only for going in. Repeat this little scenario until the pup trots right in by himself. Every time you catch him about to step into the crate, be ready to say, "Good dog—good crate." Even if he's just looking for crumbs, it means that he has accepted the idea that the crate is his own place, and that's your goal.

Open the door to let the puppy out only when he is quiet—or even asleep. Gradually increase the length of time he stays in the crate with the door closed until you reach half an hour or more. As the time increases, begin going in and out of the room, varying the amount of time you are with the puppy and are not.

The exception to this crate-training process occurs overnight. Right before you go to bed, take the puppy out to eliminate, then put him in the crate in your bedroom (at least on the first night in your home—you may want to tempt him with a small biscuit) and close the crate door. No conversation. He'll settle down if you ignore him. It's been a very busy day.

First thing in the morning—at the very first sound from the puppy—pick up the leash and the pup (or lead him, if he's too big to carry) to his spot and wait. It shouldn't take long this time.

INDOOR RULES

Once you are back indoors, don't make the common mistake of letting the puppy run free all over your

Expect your puppy to go where he's not supposed to go and get into things he's not supposed to get into if you don't confine him while you're not around.

house. That kind of freedom means only one thing: "freedom to be punished," because puppies on their own will get into trouble. Confinement to one room or one area in a room is actually being kind to your puppy.

If you can't keep an eye on him, let him relieve himself, offer fresh water and then the puppy can go into his crate, go "free" in his confined area with a couple of toys or go to sleep. Puppies need a lot of sleep because they are growing so fast.

PAPER-TRAINING

If everyone leaves the house in the morning and returns six to eight hours later, you have several options. You can ask a friend, neighbor or professional pet sitter to take the puppy out for an hour in the middle of the day (and feed him, and take him out again), or you can paper-train.

Leave several thicknesses of newspaper in one corner of the area the puppy is confined to when you are out—in one corner of an ex-pen away from his water dish and his bed, or, as an alternative, in one corner by the back door. *Warning:* If you paper the entire floor (or even too large an area), the puppy will use the entire area, probably by turning at least half of it into confetti. Boredom has a way of expressing itself.

TIPS FOR CITY DOGS

Carry a small puppy in the elevator or up and down stairs. A puppy too big to carry is still a puppy, so protect him in the elevator by letting him sit in the corner. Stand in front of him so that he won't get stepped on.

City street noises can be frightening to a puppy. Find as secluded a spot as possible in which to curb your pup. Take plastic baggies with you and do your part to keep your city clean.

On your return, take the puppy outside as usual, and clean up the newspapers in silence. That gives the pup the message that what he did is okay, but only okay, nothing to warrant either praise or disapproval.

When the time comes to do without papers, gradually diminish the papered area. Many people who must leave their adult dogs alone all day routinely put newspapers down, just in case. Better a soiled newspaper than a damaged bladder.

CHAPTER FIVE

On Good Behavior

Basic training does not wait until your puppy is 6 months old. It begins immediately. You are teaching the pup, intentionally or not, what she's allowed to do—thereby she earns your smiles and sweet talk—and what she is definitely not allowed to do. A puppy is a sponge, and spends every waking moment soaking up her environment and figuring out how all of it relates to her. (Puppies, like kids, are very "me" oriented.) Every dog needs to know her exact place within her new family circle.

DAY ONE: TOURING THE HOUSE

Begin as you mean to continue. Bring the puppy into the house and give her a complete tour on a loose leash. This is the pup's first introduction to whatever limitations you want to put on her future access to your possessions—your furniture, golf clubs, books, the kids' toy shelves.

This is not the right time to begin using the word "No!" (The puppy might begin to think that "No!" is her name!) Instead, use a guttural "aacht!" combined with a very slight tug-and-release of the leash as she sniffs to warn her away from untouchables. She's new at this, but just saying, "Puppy!" in a happy voice may be enough to get her to look at you—"Good dog." Back to happy chatter as you move on.

All you are doing is letting her know by means of prevention (a growl sound she understands) what things she will have to avoid in the future. Let her sniff first because she'll remember the objects more by scent than by sight. She looks up at you and she is praised.

TOILET TIME!

House tour is over! Now it's down to specifics. Show Alice where her water bowl will always be. Let her investigate her crate. Then take her outside (still on leash) to the exact area where you want her to eliminate. Stand there until she does. (Patience. She's new at this.) Praise quietly as she goes, after which you can make the same kind of tour outside, with warnings about flower or vegetable beds, bushes or plants.

You may live in a city and by law (and responsible dog ownership) must curb Alice. Go to the quietest

no-parking spot you can find. If you remain on the sidewalk, she will naturally want to join you, so stand down in the street with her. It will take time, plus your casual, confident attitude, to get her used to the noise, the confusion and the speed and size of trucks and taxis. No outside walking tour at this time. Wait until her immunizations are complete, by which time she will also be more accepting of city life.

Note: If the original trip home from where you picked up the puppy took more than an hour, reverse the two "tours" to let the pup eliminate first.

TEACHING BASICS

There are three basic training ingredients needed to turn your puppy into an intelligent, well-behaved, cooperative dog. They are: Confinement, Prevention and Consistency.

Confinement

INDOORS

By keeping the puppy in one safe room in your house you are doing more than just keeping her safe. Alice is learning to respect the limits you set. She is learning that

you come and go and she doesn't have to panic when she hears you pick up the car keys. She is taking in all she needs to know about her new home and doing it all from a safe vantage point—safe from her viewpoint and yours. Confinement = "Good dog."

A puppy given free run of the house is unable to learn appropriate control and boundaries. The place where you choose to confine your pup when you can't be on Puppy Patrol may be your kitchen (with pet gates in doorways) or an exercise-pen set up in any room that has destruction-free flooring. For short-term confinement, use the puppy's crate. A radio left on a "lite"

or classical music station helps prevent separation anxiety when you're out of the room, or the house. The music and occasional voices relax the puppy, and the pup that is relaxed doesn't resort to excessive barking.

OUTDOORS

Two things keep a dog safe: one is a leash, the other is a fence. As Alice grows up, you'll want her to be outdoors part of the day. If you own your own property, you have a wide choice of fencing. When considering which kind, remember that dogs dig, climb, chew and bark. (They also play, wag their tails and let us know we're the best, which are the other reasons for the fence!)

When you first bring your puppy home, give her a tour of the house on a leash to let her investigate everything in a controlled way.

THE DOG RUN—Perhaps fencing is not an option because you rent your home. A free-standing dog run is the answer for those dark and stormy nights (and equally dark early mornings) when Alice has to go out, but you'd rather stay inside, thank you! This style of dog run can be taken apart and put in the moving van when you move.

It can also be moved from a shady spot in summer to a spot right by the back door for winter. Wire tops are available to keep Super Dog from climbing out, as are awning-type tops to keep out rain, sun or snow. A run can be set up on grass, concrete or a bed of crushed stone. Note, however, that a dog run is not meant to provide real physical exercise. Alice will still need to be played with and walked.

LEAVING YOUR DOG OUTDOORS—Some breeds in some parts of the country will be kept outside all day while the owners are at work. There's no problem with doing this as long as the dog is never left tied up, which is cruel, unsafe and causes undue stress. A secure dog run with an all-weather doghouse, an adequate fresh water supply and an appropriate variety of toys will provide part of the answer. The other important part is for the first person home to bring Alice indoors to be with the family. Dogs are social animals. They need to be with people and to be part of the action.

Apartment-dwellers have no choice but to walk their dogs (after the series of puppy shots is complete) on sidewalks and in parks, which is fine by Alice.

Prevention

Prevention is the easiest, quickest and surest way to discipline (teach) your puppy. Invariably, the mischief (or, if left for more than a few minutes, full-blown destruction) that

A strong, high fence around your yard is the best way to keep your puppy safe while she's outdoors, and to ensure the goodwill of your neighbors.

36

your puppy gets into will be discovered by you long after the fact. The pup that managed to chew through the leg of the coffee table obviously had not been watched for some time.

When you finally spot the damage, you do the normal thing: You blow up! Just please don't blow up at your puppy. Shout "No!" only if Alice is still hard at work. Whether caught in the act or not, give her a time-out in her crate. During her time-out, you can repeat ten times: "I could have prevented that." You can't undo the damage, but you don't have to let it happen again. Be fair to yourself and to your puppy that doesn't know antique cherry in the dining room from a fallen branch under a tree. Wood is wood.

Here are the rules for Puppy Punishment Prevention:

- When you can't watch, crate.

- When you can't watch or crate (longer periods of time), confine.

- When Alice is "free" with you in the house, watch!

No one is perfect. No puppy is perfect. There will be mishaps, but follow the rules and you will avoid disasters.

Consistency

Your puppy hasn't even learned her own "language" and you're teaching her a foreign one, so you must be consistent. Use exactly the same word to mean exactly the same thing every time to enable the puppy to make a clear connection between the word and the desired action. Pretend she speaks a rare foreign dialect— you can't punish her for not understanding what you said!

Here's the standard example of how this works using the word "Off!" You'll be using it as a one-word command, which your pup will learn easily if you are consistent and don't confuse her. Use the one word "Off!" when you mean "Don't jump up on Aunt Martha!" and when you mean "Get off the couch!" "Off!" can also mean "Don't put your paws on the windowsill." But it is a one-word command. Your puppy will be confused (not disobedient) if you say, "Don't jump up!" one time, "Get off!" another, "Get down!" on another occasion and "Stay off!" still another.

Consistency is everything in the life of a dog. Older dogs can adjust when we change routines, but puppies thrive on knowing what to expect and when to expect it. Consistency makes you a reliable, trustworthy person. Trust is of prime importance to your puppy. If she trusts you, she will listen and learn from you.

From 3 to 6 months of age, the puppy is learning how to learn, so training sessions are tied in with fun, simply paying attention, praise and being with you. Discipline instills self-discipline and self-confidence, but puppies this age are still emotionally immature and most are sensitive to correction. Some will remain that way. Never make a harsh correction or punishment by hand, voice or leash. (Remember the foreign dialect barrier: Make yourself clear; don't punish her for not understanding what you said!)

Obedience instructors generally stick to the 6 months of age minimum for beginners based on the probability that the puppy is house-trained (most training facilities are indoors and rented), on the puppy's ability to concentrate for more than two minutes, and on the owner's capability of handling a slightly more mature, less rambunctious dog. In other words, the "6 months or older" rule prevents chaos in the average canine classroom.

NURSERY SCHOOL BEGINS

At 3 to 5 months of age all puppies are more or less equal in everything but size, and that difference isn't a problem to the pups. Puppy Kindergarten offers you instruction in basic grooming techniques and use of the collar and leash; if you happen to know all that, the socialization of your puppy is the best reason to attend.

A puppy that was in a litter of one or two, or a puppy that was taken from her littermates at a very young age, needs to be reminded how to behave around dogs. All of them learn how to interact safely with other pups, how to greet each other, how to play, how to "read" canine body language, how to respond to their own name and to their own special person and how to greet the strangers who belong to those other puppies. The "graduates" then go on to pre-Beginner or Beginner obedience classes at 6 months of age, or after a short break.

WHAT EVERY DOG NEEDS TO KNOW

There are six standard commands: "Heel," "Come," "Sit," "Stand,"

"Stay" and "Down." With a new puppy, it doesn't matter too much where you begin. Training sessions should last only two to five minutes, which is approximately the length of your pup's attention span. The important thing is to practice every day and never to be in any hurry to go to the next lesson. You do not set the pace for learning, your puppy does.

Rewards

Rewards come in three forms: treats, pats and verbal praise. To grade your "student's" qualification for a reward, consider a treat the equivalent of an "A," a pat a "B" and verbal praise a "C." Any two together equal an A+, so be very careful not to go overboard or you'll run out of appropriate compensation and the pup will quit!

Verbal praise has a range from ecstatic (for the first few correct responses from a very young pup) to a calm "Good dog!" as the dog grows up and becomes more expert. Don't overuse food treats when practicing. As each word command is fully learned, gradually cut back on the treats and substitute "Good dog!" or just a big smile. (An "A+"

The best way to train your puppy is to make sure that the training sessions are fun—for you as well as your puppy!

39

will retain its impact all the way through college, as will "ecstatic.")

TEACHING "HEEL"

Heeling is not the same as going for a walk. When your dog heels, you do not want her to be smelling the flowers, or lifting a leg on every hydrant. Heeling is an obedience exercise in which the dog stays close beside you, paying attention only to you and where you are going.

As your puppy grows up, heeling will become the safe way for you to walk your dog through crowds and across streets, ignoring distractions. Begin by getting the pup's attention as she's trotting along next to you; you want to make her conscious of what she is doing.

Hold her attention by walking just quickly enough to make the puppy want to keep up with you. If she's not paying attention, stop and begin again—do not correct her.

PRACTICING

You can practice anywhere, anytime, on or off leash. As you notice Alice walking next to you—from fridge to stove, or across the room—take advantage of the opportunity to get in a speedy, "Let's go! Good dog!" Be realistic in what you expect of a puppy. A few steps on command earn a reward. A few more steps earn a reward. A week later Alice is heeling nicely? Praise and quit practicing immediately! Practice again later.

Add some right turns for variety and to be sure she's really paying attention. As you make the turn, bend over and clap your hands to keep her on course. Left turns take a little more expertise. Put your left foot in front of the pup to gently guide her into the turn. Careful, or you'll step on the pup and she won't think this game is very much fun! However, if your left foot happens to bump the puppy, or she plows into it, don't apologize. If she thinks it was her mistake, she'll learn to pay closer attention. Repeat the "Watch me!" signal.

TEACHING "SIT"

The "Sit" command is an easy way to have your puppy show off her good manners. A "Sit" is especially good for little everyday things, like having her leash attached.

The command is "Alice, Sit." You may have noticed that all commands are preceded by the dog's name; by doing so, you get her attention so she knows you aren't talking to someone else. Puppies are proud to have a name. It's when they reach adolescence (the terrible teens) that they, like other teenagers we all know, pretend they don't hear you. Any time you see the puppy about to sit, quickly say, "Sit—Good dog!" If she is already sitting nicely give her a "Good sit!" reward.

The easiest way to teach a young pup to sit is to get her attention with a treat held in front of and just above her nose to make her look up. Then slowly move the treat backward over her head. Because a dog wants to keep her eye on the goodie, her backside will have to drop to the floor. It takes a little practice (on your part, too) but it's a tried and true means of getting an unforced "Sit." As she assumes the position, give the command, "Alice, Sit" and hand out a tiny portion of the treat. This technique constitutes motivational teaching. The puppy performs the desired action by herself.

An alternative method of teaching a puppy to sit is to have the pup beside you (left side), hold a treat in front of her with your right hand and gently press down on her hindquarters with your left hand. With a large pup, you could put your left arm around her hindquarters and with a gentle forward motion, bend her knees, forcing the "Sit." And, as you are coping with all that, brightly say, "Alice, Sit."

THE RELEASE

When the puppy is learning each of the commands "Sit," "Down," "Stand" and "Stay," it is important that you teach her how you will release her from remaining in that position forever. The usual release is a simple "Okay!" while clapping your hands to regain the dog's attention. (Even puppies like applause.) Now's the time to love her up and tell her how utterly fabulous she is.

TEACHING "COME"

Teaching a young puppy to come when called starts off perfectly. The puppy learns her name and that people use it when they want to give her something fabulous like dinner or a new toy, so she comes running. Well, she soon learns it isn't a perfect world. She may hear her name called for a detested nail trim or to come in from outdoors just when she's having fun or enjoying a nap.

Undoubtedly the most frequent mistake people make with this command is to say "Alice, Come" when there is no possible way to enforce it. Remember consistency? The puppy only has to disobey a few

Using a food lure to teach "Sit," "Down" and "Stand."

1) "Phoenix, Sit."

2) Hand palm upwards, move lure up and back over dog's muzzle.

3) "Good sit, Phoenix!"

4) "Phoenix, Down."

5) Hand palm downwards, move lure down to lie between dog's forepaws.

6) "Phoenix, Off. Good down, Phoenix!"

7) "Phoenix, Sit!"

8) Palm upwards, move lure up and back, keeping it close to dog's muzzle.

9) "Good sit, Phoenix!"

42

10) *"Phoenix, Stand!"*
11) *Move lure away from dog at nose height, then lower it a tad.*
12) *"Phoenix, Off! Good stand, Phoenix!"*

13) *"Phoenix, Down!"*
14) *Hand palm downwards, move lure down to lie between dog's forepaws.*
15) *"Phoenix, Off! Good down-stay, Phoenix!"*

43

16) *"Phoenix, Stand!"*
17) *Move lure away from dog's muzzle up to nose height.*
18) *"Phoenix, Off! Good stand-stay, Phoenix."*

times when she hears "Alice, Come" and you have taught her that she has an option. She can come, or not. Never give her that choice. Only call "Come" if the puppy is on her way into your outstretched arms, or on leash so you can guide her toward you. This rule is in effect until your adult dog is "proofed" (tested by many diverse distractions) at 2 years of age.

"Come" is one of the primary safety signals, and therefore your goal must be 100 percent compliance. In any type of emergency involving you or your dog, you must be able to rely on A+ obedience for "Come" and "Stay." (Straight A's will do for responses to the other requests!)

TEACHING "STAND"

When you give a dog any command, you have automatically assumed a dominant role and put the dog into a submissive one. Standing is a somewhat dominant canine posture, whereas the "Sit" and the "Down" are submissive canine positions, so it is sometimes difficult to teach a naturally submissive puppy to "Stand" when told. Given the command "Stand," many dogs will obey, but quickly lower their tails, ears and head, demonstrating submissive body language. Be gentle and patient. A perfect puppy "Stand" has four feet on the ground (that's the hard part), but it's also nice to see the head up and the tail wagging. Don't worry if at first your puppy would rather be a clown than stand still. Eventually they all grow up.

Puppies do not spend much time standing around, so you'll have to teach her, not just rely on trying to catch her in the act. One way is to walk her into a "Stand." When she's pretty good at heeling, slow down and as you come to a stop, bring your right hand in front of her (palm side toward her nose) as you say "Stand." Perform this hand signal gently or your puppy will think she's going to be zonked and she'll duck!

Practice by taking one or two slow steps (without a "Let's go" command) followed by a "Stand" command. Getting that head held high and happy and the tail wagging calls for a treat poised for a moment with a "Watch me!" A couple of reasonable or good "Stands" are followed by a rousing romp in the early days of training. Standing still is very hard.

Using a toy to teach "Sit-Heel-Sit" sequences: 1) "Phoenix, Sit!" Standing still, move lure up and back over dog's muzzle . . . 2) to position dog sitting in heel position on your left side. 3) Say "Phoenix, Heel!" and walk ahead, wagging lure in left hand. Change lure to right hand in preparation for sit signal. Say "Sit" and then . . . 4) use hand signal to lure dog to sit as you stop. Eventually, dog will sit automatically at heel whenever you stop. 5) "Good dog!"

A perfect "Stand" is only required of an adult dog for about a minute. Standing is necessary for at least part of her weekly grooming, but not standing at attention. In fact, during every grooming session you can make use of "Sit," "Stand" and "Down." What a clever puppy!

TEACHING "DOWN"

"Down" is as low as your puppy can get, and it is difficult for some puppies to accept. With the puppy in a "Sit" position, hold a treat in the fingers of your right hand (let her sniff it or see it), run that hand in front of her nose, down and out toward your feet. Be prepared to use your left hand on her shoulders only if necessary to guide her into the "Down" position, which is flat on her tummy with front legs flat out in front. Deliver the treat and a "Good down!" and release.

When the puppy can do a "Down" all by herself in response to "Alice, Down," you can skip the treat intermittently, begin to add a "Stay" and gradually—very gradually—work up to a "Down" of one minute. As she matures, she'll be able to stay down for five minutes (or more if necessary), but even one minute is an eternity for an active pup, and you need to remain within a foot or two to start the exercise over again should she get up.

TIMING

Mastering good timing is probably the most challenging part of training. Your puppy connects her action with your word command only at the precise instant they come together. Timing is vital. What you say is only as effective as when you say it. When you give a puppy a command as she just happens to do something on her own, your timing is perfect.

To teach "Come," call your dog, open your arms as a welcoming signal, wave a toy or a treat and praise for every step in your direction.

CHAPTER SIX

To Good Health

Maintaining good health means being able to read the first signs of an impending health problem in order to take prompt action. A major part of canine health care lies in prevention, which includes regular veterinary care, quality food and regular grooming.

It is sometimes easy to be mystified or confused by veterinary terms that may in fact refer to a mild canine ailment. The information you will find in these pages will not replace the need for your veterinarian! But it will let you become familiar with many of those terms as well as some of the more common canine health problems, which in turn will help you communicate with your puppy's veterinarian.

KNOW YOUR PUPPY

As you watch your puppy in order to fend off mischief (and disaster), you will also be observing what is normal for your particular puppy—what he usually looks like: eyes, mouth, ears, body posture, energy level; how he behaves or reacts and how much he eats and drinks (and eliminates) on a normal day-to-day basis. This casual observation will enable you to notice when something is wrong, when he's "just not himself" or has a runny nose, when he's limping slightly on one leg and so on.

CHOOSING A VETERINARIAN

Choosing a veterinarian is difficult if you are new to pet ownership or if you've moved into a new area. One way to start is by asking friends and neighbors of their experiences with local veterinarians, keeping in mind what kind of pets they have and how their ideas of pet care coincide (or collide) with your own.

You have many types of services to choose from—and having made a choice, you need never feel bound by it. Feel free to call and ask if you may visit the offices. If the answer is "no," you wouldn't feel welcome with your dog in tow. The perfect time to get to know a veterinarian and to establish the necessary confidence in the veterinarian, the staff and the way the office is run, is when getting your puppy's inoculations. If you are not completely happy with your choice, as you become involved in the world of dogs—at training classes, for example—you'll meet others with whom you can discuss other veterinarians.

You are the vital link between your dog and his doctor. The dog can't say what is bothering him or how he feels, so you must be able to communicate to the veterinarian how the dog's current actions (eating, eliminating, sleeping and general behavior) differ from what is normal for your particular dog. If you are unable to have such an open conversation, feel cut off or sense hostility or impatience, go elsewhere.

On the other side of the coin, you have to listen to what the veterinarian is saying, watch what he or she is showing you to do and follow instructions to the letter. Many a good veterinarian has to cope with a good dog whose owner just doesn't pay attention.

PREVENTIVE CARE

The easiest way to make sure your dog is well cared for is to establish a routine and follow it every day.

For optimal health, your puppy needs high-quality dog food, fresh clean water, exercise and sleep (see chapter 2). He needs these things every day, in varying amounts, as he grows older. Nutrition-related defects occur from both overfeeding and surplus vitamins as well as from too little nutrition. "Environmental stress" refers to subjecting a growing

48

puppy to excessive activities such as jogging, running or overly long walks, all of which should be avoided until growth is complete.

Beyond this basic care, take the time, every day, to run your hands over your puppy. You can do this while you're grooming him. But don't just pet and brush him; instead, run your fingers through and under the coat so that you can feel the dog's skin. As you do this, you will get to know the feel of your dog. Should he pick up a tick, you will feel it with your fingers. If he has a cut, a lump, a bruise or a skin rash, you will feel it.

By checking the dog like this every day, you will find minor problems before they become serious. When you start this routine in puppyhood, your dog will come to love it, and will be more accepting of being petted by other people—especially the veterinarian—as an adult.

The best time for this physical exam is after you have brushed your puppy. Start at his head and, using your fingertips to navigate through the fur, feel all over your puppy's head, including around his muzzle, eyes, ears and neck. Take your time and be gentle; think of it as giving your puppy a massage.

Run your hands regularly over your dog to feel for any injuries.

49

Continue working your hands down your puppy's body, examining his shoulders, back, sides, legs and tail. Run your hands down each leg, handling each toe on each paw, checking for burrs and foxtails, cuts and scratches. If you find any minor cuts and scrapes, you can wash them off with soap and water and apply a mild antibiotic ointment. However, if a cut is gaping or looks red and inflamed, call your veterinarian. Check your puppy's tummy, too. Fleas like to hide in the groin area and behind elbows—don't miss those spots.

Once you've checked his entire body this way, return to his head. It's time to check your puppy's mouth, looking for inflamed gums, foreign objects or possible cracked or broken teeth. Become familiar with what the teeth look like, inside and out. This is a good time to brush the teeth. Next, clean the inside of the ears, as described in chapter 3.

Check your puppy's nails. They need regular trimming, but not every day. However, a daily check will keep you posted on whether any nails are chipped or cracked.

A healthy puppy is active, alert and ready to go when awake, but because rapid growth is tiring, long naps are normal. Note that there is a difference between a "nicely filled-out puppy" and one with a "big fat tummy." The latter (a swollen or distended stomach) is more likely to be caused by roundworms than by overeating.

YOUR PUPPY'S TEMPERATURE

The temperature of a healthy puppy ranges from 101° to 102.5° Fahrenheit taken with a rectal thermometer.

To take the pup's temperature yourself, shake down a rectal thermometer until it reads about 95°, then put a dab of petroleum jelly on the tip and, holding the pup's tail with one hand (so he won't sit down), insert it gently with a slight twisting motion about 1 inch into the rectum. Hold it for at least a minute (three minutes is best, but that's a long time for a pup). Any reading over 103° is cause for calling the veterinarian.

WHEN TO CALL THE VETERINARIAN

Base your puppy's health on the rule of "better safe than sorry." If you are unsure of anything concerning the health of your puppy, call your veterinarian's office. If the condition is not serious—something every puppy goes through—a certified technician on staff can probably provide you with adequate help. If the matter warrants veterinary examination and/or treatment, you'll be advised of that, too.

Always remember that your veterinarian is practicing preventive medicine. He or she needs your help in order to make it work for your puppy. Here are some typical problems that would warrant calling the veterinarian:

1. Diarrhea or vomiting that lasts more than one day. Call immediately if the contents of either one are dark or contain blood.

2. Complete loss of appetite for more than a day.

3. A fever above 103°, or shivering in a warm room.

4. Seizure or convulsions.

5. Choking, coughing or raspy breath.

6. Any sudden change in water consumption, urination or general behavior that lasts for more than one day.

7. Limping that does not improve after one day of complete rest (crate confinement) or any lameness that is painful.

8. Runny nose, watery eyes.

9. Drooling or slobbering (from a dog that doesn't normally do either).

IMMUNIZATIONS

Healthy puppies, in order to stay healthy, need to be immunized against several potentially lethal diseases. The vaccinations your puppy has had, and may be given in the next few weeks, are often referred to as "puppy shots" or "temporary immunizations," which might lead you to believe that the final shots in the series of these protective vaccines are "permanent." They are not!

An annual routine checkup by your veterinarian will include the administration of "booster shots," which are adult updates of puppy shots. These vaccinations are an essential part of keeping your dog healthy.

Schedule of Puppy Shots

Breeders will generally have seen to it that their puppies have had their first set of shots, sometimes even the second set, depending upon the puppy's age at the time of sale. From then on it is the owner's responsibility to follow a schedule set by the veterinarian. The complete series is usually given at 8, 10 and 12 weeks of age.

These first immunizations, or puppy shots, are often given as one injection and include distemper, hepatitis, leptospirosis, parainfluenza and parvovirus vaccine. Known simply (and gratefully!) as "DHLPP," it is first given at about 8 weeks of age. The next shots may add "C" for coronavirus if advisable in your area.

DISTEMPER—Distemper is a very contagious viral disease that used to

51

Immunizations will help protect your puppy from the most common canine diseases.

kill thousands of puppies. Today's vaccines are extremely effective, but puppies still die from it.

Symptoms of this disease are weakness and depression, a fever and a discharge from the eyes and nose. Infected puppies cough, vomit and have diarrhea. Intravenous fluids and antibiotics may help support an infected dog, but unfortunately, most dogs with distemper die.

INFECTIOUS HEPATITIS—This is a highly contagious virus that primarily attacks the liver but can also cause severe kidney damage. Initial symptoms include depression, vomiting, abdominal pain, high fever and jaundice. Mild cases may be treated with intravenous fluids,

antibiotics and even blood transfusions; however, the mortality rate is very high.

LEPTOSPIROSIS—Leptospirosis is a bacterial disease spread by the urine of infected wildlife. If your puppy drinks from a contaminated stream or sniffs at a bush that has been urinated on by an infected animal, he may pick up the bacteria. The bacteria attacks the kidneys, causing kidney failure. Symptoms include fever, loss of appetite, possible diarrhea and jaundice.

PARVOVIRUS—Parvovirus, or parvo as it is commonly known, attacks the inner lining of the intestines, causing bloody diarrhea that has a distinct odor. It is a terrible killer of puppies and is extremely contagious. In puppies under 10 weeks of age, the virus also attacks the heart, causing death, often with no other symptoms. The virus moves rapidly and dehydration can lead to shock and death in a matter of hours.

CORONAVIRUS—Coronavirus is rarely fatal to adult dogs, although it is frequently fatal to puppies. The symptoms of a coronavirus infection include vomiting, loss of appetite and a yellowish, watery stool that might contain mucus or blood. The stools carry the shed virus, which is highly contagious.

PARAINFLUENZA (KENNEL COUGH)—This respiratory infection can be caused by any number of different viral or bacterial agents. These highly contagious, airborne agents can cause a variety of symptoms, including inflammation of the trachea, bronchi and lungs, as well as mild to severe coughing. Antibiotics may be prescribed to combat or prevent pneumonia and a cough suppressant may quiet the cough. Fortunately, the disease is usually mild and many puppies

YOUR PUPPY'S VACCINES

Vaccines are given to prevent your dog from getting an infectious disease like canine distemper or rabies. Vaccines are the ultimate preventive medicine. That's why it is necessary for your dog to be vaccinated routinely. Puppy vaccines start at 8 weeks of age for the five-in-one DHLPP vaccine. Your veterinarian will put your puppy on a proper schedule and should remind you when to bring in your dog for shots.

recover quickly without any treatment at all.

RABIES—Rabies is a highly infectious virus usually carried by wildlife, especially bats, raccoons and skunks. Any warm-blooded animal, including humans, can be infected. The virus is transmitted by the infected animal's saliva, through a bite or break in the skin. It then travels up to the brain and spinal cord and throughout the body.

Behavior changes are the first sign of the disease. As the virus spreads, the animal will have trouble swallowing and will drool or salivate excessively. Paralysis and convulsions follow.

The rabies vaccine is routinely given to pups at 6 months of age in most parts of the United States. Most of these vaccines will remain effective for three years.

INTERNAL PARASITES

ROUNDWORM—Roundworm is a very common internal parasite in young puppies. Take a fresh stool sample on your first visit to the veterinarian so it can be checked for worms. Roundworms are easy to treat, but can cause serious problems if left untreated. Don't try to treat roundworm yourself because the "cure" is actually a poison to kill the worms that could harm your puppy if incorrectly administered.

HOOKWORM—Hookworm eggs burrow into the skin through a puppy's feet or are acquired by eating an infected animal's stools. In the body, hookworms migrate to the dog's small intestines, where

they latch on and suck blood. When the worms detach and move, they leave open wounds behind, causing bloody diarrhea—the first sign of infection. People can also contract hookworm from infected soil.

WHIPWORM—Whipworms feed on blood in the large intestine, and a heavy infestation leaves a puppy looking thin, usually with watery or bloody diarrhea. Whipworm eggs can live in soil for many years and can be acquired by eating new grass, digging up a bone or licking the dirt.

TAPEWORM—Tapeworms grow in the dog's intestines, where they absorb nutrients from the intestinal wall. They are acquired by swallowing fleas, the intermediary host. You can tell if your dog has tapeworms by noticing white rice-like segments in his feces. These are the segments of growing tapeworms.

HEARTWORM—Heartworm infestation is passed on to the dog by a bite from a mosquito, which is the intermediary host between infected animals. The worm itself grows in the chambers of the heart and is almost always fatal. The treatment involves the use of arsenic to kill

Common internal parasites (l-r): roundworm, whipworm, tapeworm and hookworm.

the heartworm, itself a dangerous procedure.

Heartworm preventative in the form of a pill is given every day or every thirty days, depending on which type you choose, but only after your veterinarian has obtained a negative result from a preliminary blood test that must be done annually. When the medication is started and how long it is continued depends on the incidence of heartworm in your area.

SPAY/NEUTER

Myths abound on the subject of spaying (for females) and neutering (for males), but the facts are plain and simple: It is extremely beneficial to your pet's health. Either operation is performed when the pup is about 6 months of age, or just approaching sexual maturity, but discuss with your veterinarian the best time for your puppy. It is a minor operation from which the pup recovers quickly. The major benefit is that you, as a responsible pet owner, will have eliminated any chance of adding to the overpopulation of unwanted puppies.

Spaying involves the removal of the uterus, tubes and ovaries. Spaying

ADVANTAGE OF SPAYING/NEUTERING

The greatest advantage of spaying (for females) or neutering (for males) your dog is that you are guaranteed that your dog will not produce puppies. There are too many puppies already available for too few homes. There are other advantages as well.

Advantages of Spaying

No messy heats.

No "suitors" howling at your windows or waiting in your yard.

Eliminates possibility of pyometra (disease of the uterus) and decreases the incidence of breast cancer.

Advantages of Neutering

Lessens male aggressive and territorial behaviors, but doesn't affect the dog's personality.

Prevents the need to roam in search of bitches in season.

Decreased incidences of urogenital diseases.

eliminates the likelihood of the most common cancers in bitches (mammary and uterine) by an estimated 95 percent. Your bitch will not become obese after the procedure unless you overfeed her and don't provide her with sufficient exercise.

55

FIGHTING FLEAS

Remember, the fleas you see on your dog are only part of the problem—the smallest part! To rid your dog and home of fleas, you need to treat your dog and your home. Here's how:

- Identify where your pet(s) sleep. These are "hot spots."

- Clean your pets' bedding, your own floors and furniture regularly by vacuuming and washing.

- Spray "hot spots" with a nontoxic, long-lasting flea larvicide.

- Treat outdoor "hot spots" with insecticide.

- Kill eggs on pets with a product containing insect growth regulators (IGRs).

- Kill fleas on pets per your veterinarian's recommendation.

Neutering, or the removal of both testicles in the male dog, not only eliminates unwanted offspring, but also diminishes the dog's desire to "mark" or urinate on everything

The flea is a die-hard pest.

that stands upright. It even reduces the normally strong odor of male urine. It will not turn your pup into a wimp, or change his personality—except perhaps to calm aggressive outbursts when encountering other male dogs. He will still protect you and be as good a watchdog as ever. Neutering will not cause him to get fat. Overfeeding and under-exercising, however, will.

FLEAS

Fleas are a prolific, common environmental enemy of people and animals. Despite the number of products on the market to rid the dog, the house and the garden of this pest, the flea continues to thrive.

The first thing to do is accept the fact that if you discover one flea on your pet, your house probably contains thousands of fleas in various stages of growth. Treating the dog will make him more comfortable temporarily, and spraying him with one of the new insect growth regulators will inhibit further growth of eggs or larvae on the dog or when they drop off onto your carpet. However, you must thoroughly clean and de-flea your house and your yard.

TICKS

Ticks are rapidly catching up with fleas in many areas of the country as the most invasive insect, especially the tiny deer ticks (found on whitetail deer and white-footed mice) that are the carriers of Lyme disease, which infects dogs and humans.

To Remove a Tick

Saturate a cotton ball with alcohol, nail-polish remover (acetone) or even gin. Dab the tick with the soaked cotton ball. This will stun it, causing it to lose its grip. Wait a few seconds, then, using tweezers held close to the skin, with a steady, firm pull draw the tick out. The blood of an engorged tick is as dangerous to you as to your dog, so try not to crush the tick.

If you're squeamish, there's a small plastic device called a Tick-Pick (in pet stores) that is easy to use. Dispose of the tick (or take it to your veterinarian for testing if you think it's a deer tick and your dog has not been immunized). Clean the area with an antiseptic and wash your hands thoroughly. Most flea repellents also deter ticks.

Use tweezers to remove ticks from your dog.

PROBLEMS OF THE MUSCULOSKELETAL SYSTEM

You can prevent some harm to a puppy's bones and joints that is due to such things as excessive or inappropriate activity, an inadequate diet or accidental trauma. A playful puppy should not be encouraged to fly off a step like "Super Puppy," which can result in impaired bone growth, injured joints or strained muscles. Injury can also result indoors from a puppy sliding on a slippery, highly waxed floor. Some of this damage may be permanent, if only as the seat of arthritis in later years.

While there are serious reasons for a puppy to limp, the most

57

frequent are apt to be a pulled muscle, minor injury to a toe or nail or a foreign object caught in or between the pads of a foot. Check out those possibilities first. With crate rest and "necessary" trips outside kept brief and on leash, the puppy should show improvement in a day or two.

Dogs don't complain about pain or discomfort, and will summon every bit of physical and mental strength to keep up with you and meet your demands. This makes your evaluation of health situations difficult. If the dog exhibits pain in trying to get up or lie down, or when you touch a particular area, he needs to be looked at by your veterinarian.

RESPIRATORY PROBLEMS

The respiratory system of the dog has a different range of sounds from that of people. For example, there's sneezing that sounds like choking, coughing that sounds like a goose honking, sniffing or snuffling at everything. These differences are most noticeable in the brachycephalic, or short-nosed, dogs.

Kennel Cough

Kennel cough is serious in puppies, but less so in adult dogs. However, it is highly contagious and the dog must be kept isolated. It is characterized by a dry, harsh, hacking cough and occasionally a runny nose (especially in puppies), but otherwise the dog will seem to be healthy and bright.

Most cases are mild, lasting about two weeks. The dog needs a warm room and a vaporizer, preferably the cold-steam type. Take the dog's temperature daily. An elevated temperature indicates the presence of something more serious than kennel cough. For a persistent dry cough, a cough suppressant may be given, but check with your vet as to which product is suitable for your dog and the correct dosage. Keep in touch with your veterinarian, because bronchitis can develop from the original infection.

Kennel cough vaccine (given as a nasal spray) is a good precaution for every puppy going into kindergarten puppy training, for dogs in any training classes or just for play-dates in the park. It is a requirement of all well-run boarding kennels.

A puppy with kennel cough must be kept isolated from other dogs.

Pneumonia

Pneumonia is an infection of the lungs that can result from the kennel cough virus, but in puppies pneumonia is primarily the bacterial type. There are several other types of pneumonia, but all are characterized by a high temperature, coughing, rapid breathing and pulse and the telltale "rattling" sounds in the chest. This is serious. Get to the veterinarian immediately!

PROBLEMS OF THE EYES, EARS AND MOUTH

Eyes

Any change in the appearance of the eyes—watering, dryness, itching, redness, discharge, color—calls for a prompt visit to the vet. Sight is very precious and minor problems that can be easily corrected can just as easily worsen if left untreated.

Ears

A dog's hearing is far more sensitive than a human's; they have the ability to hear an added range of high-frequency sounds. That's why we rely on the dog to be our first alert. Dogs' ears must be kept clean and free of mites, dirt, excessive wax and hair. Wipe each ear with a separate cotton ball that has been slightly dampened in warm water. Use a cotton swab to clean the sides of the outer ear canal, but be wary of pushing debris down into the canal. If

Your puppy's eyes should be bright and full of life.

you aren't sure, ask your veterinarian or groomer to show you how to clean your dog's ears. Healthy ears smell clean.

Infections in the ear, when caught in time, are easily treated. Do not try to treat an ear infection yourself—you could damage the ear canal.

Mites are the common cause of most ear problems. Let your veterinarian diagnose the problem and show you how to treat it.

Mouth

In order to avoid infection, it is essential to keep any folds of skin around the mouth clean and free of food—easily taken care of when brushing the dog's teeth, a task described in detail later in this chapter.

Foreign objects in the mouth must be removed immediately; however, it isn't always easy to do. Care must always be taken not to push a foreign object down the throat. Hook your finger behind the object so that you are pulling it forward. But that, of course, means you are pulling from a broader area into a narrower one. As you can see, this condition can quickly turn into an emergency. If the object goes down the throat, or you can't dislodge it, get to your veterinarian immediately.

When the obstruction is already lodged in the throat, the signs of distress will include slobbering and an inability to swallow without pain or discomfort, accompanied by what may appear to be attempts to "cough up" the object. Take immediate action.

Brushing your dog's teeth is another "must." Do it as part of the grooming routine, plus two or three times more during the week. The easiest way is to use a canine toothbrush and toothpaste. (Do not use people toothpaste since a dog doesn't spit it out and it can cause stomach upsets.) A small puppy has no problem letting you put your finger in his mouth, and this method can be continued, using a gauze pad wrapped around your finger and dipped in (dog) toothpaste or a baking soda and water paste. Lift the lip gently and rub the outsides and gumline of all the teeth. Some dogs enjoy having their mouth sprayed with plain water when the brushing is over.

Your dog will still need to have his teeth examined at least once a year, and preferably professionally cleaned, by the veterinarian to keep the teeth, gums and mouth healthy. If routine care is overlooked, gingivitis and periodontitis (and bad breath) are likely to develop—just like in people!

GASTROINTESTINAL PROBLEMS

Intestinal upsets, whether an actual disease or infection, or from having eaten forbidden food, are all too common in puppies. Everything that is in reach goes into the mouth and ends up in the stomach! If you know when unauthorized food went down, you'll know to watch for constipation or diarrhea.

More serious is the swallowed object that is not food, but a toy, piece of plastic, metal or cloth, because such items can lodge in the

intestinal tract and require surgery to remove.

Gastrointestinal upsets are among the easiest health problems to recognize because the symptoms are diarrhea or constipation, excessive drinking and urinating and/or vomiting. In some cases the puppy will otherwise appear to be healthy, but usually the dog's body language is "down": ears held back and down, tail down and head down.

Constipation may be caused by any indigestible thing a dog eats or by a lack of fiber in the diet. A dog normally defecates two to four times a day, so if an entire day goes by without the dog passing stool (or passing watery or bloody stool), he is constipated. Your veterinarian will

Most gastrointestinal upsets result when a puppy's curiosity gets the best of him and he ingests something that he shouldn't.

want to see the dog if the problem doesn't clear up in twenty-four to forty-eight hours.

Diarrhea is a common symptom of many conditions, ranging from a minor digestive upset to extremely serious disease. At the onset of diarrhea or very loose stools, withhold food (but not water) for a day, but contact your veterinarian immediately. He may suggest a "people remedy"—Kaopectate or Pepto-Bismol—but don't give it without a veterinarian's instructions, as the dosage depends on the size and age of your dog.

Other, more serious diseases of which diarrhea is a symptom include coccidia, giardia and worms, all intestinal parasites and treatable given prompt attention.

Vomiting is something dogs seem to do easily and often without a verifiable reason. For example, dogs often vomit after eating grass—to a point where it is thought they may eat grass in order to vomit! If your dog vomits more than a few times, or heaves without ejecting anything more than clear or yellow liquid, get on the phone to the veterinarian. If the vomiting is in conjunction with any other symptom, such as diarrhea or pain, it is a serious condition and must be professionally treated.

URINARY TRACT PROBLEMS

A urinary tract disorder should be suspected if your housetrained dog loses control and begins to wet anywhere and everywhere in the house, tries to void but appears to be in pain or drinks the water bowl dry no matter how often you fill it. Any such abnormality is reason for you to contact the veterinarian. The quicker a diagnosis is made and treatment begun, the less chance there is for the condition to become more serious (kidney failure, for example) and therefore more difficult to treat.

FIRST AID AND EMERGENCIES

Your puppy cannot tell you when he is sick, but if you spend enough time with him and are observant of his behavior, you'll notice when he's feeling off. The following are examples of problems that require first aid.

First aid is what you do to assist a dog in an emergency situation before you reach the veterinarian's office. Such assistance should be minimal, so as not to exacerbate the problem, and it must be safe for the dog and his rescuer. If possible, alert the veterinarian immediately.

The first rule of canine first aid is for the rescuer to remain completely calm and (outwardly at least) in control of the situation. The second rule is to fight off the desire to pick up or lean over to comfort a hurt dog face-to-face the way you would a child. When hurt and frightened, a dog's instinct for self-preservation takes over; he is likely to bite whatever comes near. That's where safety comes in.

In an Emergency

If something happens to your puppy during nonregular veterinary visiting hours, it's important to have an emergency number to call. Ask your veterinarian for this number on your first visit and keep it by the phone. You won't want to be scrambling for it when a real emergency strikes. And you won't want to be struggling with directions in the middle of the night if you've never been to the emergency clinic before. It's a good idea to do a practice run to the emergency clinic during a nonemergency. You'll need

A First-Aid Kit

Keep a canine first-aid kit on hand for general care and emergencies. Check it periodically to make sure liquids haven't spilled or dried up, and replace medications and materials after they're used. Your kit should include:

- Activated charcoal tablets
- Adhesive tape (1 and 2 inches wide)
- Antibacterial ointment (for skin and eyes)
- Aspirin (buffered or enteric coated, not Ibuprofen or acetaminophen)
- Bandages: gauze rolls (1 and 2 inches wide) and dressing pads
- Cotton balls
- Diarrhea medicine
- Dosing syringe
- Hydrogen peroxide (3%)
- Petroleum jelly
- Rectal thermometer
- Rubber gloves
- Rubbing alcohol
- Scissors
- Tourniquet
- Towel
- Tweezers

63

all the calm you can muster in a real emergency, and knowing how long it will take to get to the clinic is important.

Typical First-Aid Situations

When you notice anything unusual in the way your puppy is acting, ask yourself these questions:

- What was your first clue there was something wrong?

- Is your puppy eating normally?

- Does your puppy have a temperature? (Instructions on how to take your puppy's temperature are provided earlier in this chapter.)

- What do your puppy's stools look like?

- Is your puppy limping?

- When you do a hands-on exam, is your puppy sore anywhere? Can you feel a lump? Is anything red or swollen?

Write down anything you've noticed. When you call your veterinarian, be prepared to give specific details.

RESTRAINTS

Having established the fact that injured dogs bite, be certain that the dog is breathing normally before attempting to muzzle him. Limited breathing could be made worse by keeping the dog's mouth closed. Don't have a muzzle handy? No problem. A necktie, pantyhose, 2 feet of rope or a dog leash will do nicely. Tie a loose knot in the middle and slip the loop of the knot over the middle of the dog's nose. Pull it firm and tie the two ends under the dog's chin, then in back of the dog's ears. (Make that last tie a bow so it will untie easily to pull forward and off the nose.)

SHOCK

Many things, from dehydration to poisoning, can cause a dog to go

Use a scarf or old hose to make a temporary muzzle.

64

into shock, but being hit by a car is the most common cause of canine shock. Since "shock" refers to the breakdown of the cardiovascular system, immediate veterinary care is essential.

Electrical shock is the fate of a puppy left to chew on an electric cord his owner forgot to put up out of reach. The result is a nasty burn to the mouth which, while painful, will heal in time. More serious are lightning strikes or touching downed wires, as in either case the dog (if not killed) is burned and also suffers circulatory (heart) collapse and pulmonary (lung) edema. If the dog is unconscious and not breathing, give artificial respiration. No matter what the condition, get to a veterinarian immediately.

Hit by Car

Automobiles still account for most canine deaths, which is a sad commentary on our responsible dog ownership. All it takes to keep your dog safe is a leash or a fence and basic obedience training. No matter how slight the injury may seem, any dog hit by a car requires immediate emergency treatment by a veterinarian. There may be internal injuries or bleeding, broken bones or concussion. (See "Shock," above.)

Check for external bleeding and stop it by applying a pressure bandage or just holding a bandage or clean padded cloth over the wound. Spurting blood indicates a severed artery, which can also be controlled by applying pressure on the artery.

Moving an injured dog other than a very small one requires two people and a board (bench, sled or any improvised stretcher) or a blanket held taut. Do not muzzle a dog in shock, but keep the dog quiet and transfer him immediately to the veterinarian's office.

When a board is the means of transportation, be sure the dog is securely tied to it with strips of sheeting or rope. An injured animal panics easily and could do himself further damage in struggling to escape.

Life-Saving Procedures

There are several procedures that you should know how to perform that could instantly save your dog's life. Artificial respiration, to start the dog breathing again, and heart massage, used when no heartbeat can be felt or heard, together

65

form the well-known CPR (cardiopulmonary resuscitation). The Heimlich maneuver is the method used to dislodge a foreign object that is causing the dog to choke.

CHEST COMPRESSION

The easiest way to administer artificial respiration is by compressing the chest. Here is the five-step method for chest compression:

1. Feel or listen for a pulse or heartbeat.

2. Clear the mouth of secretions and foreign objects. (You might have to use the Heimlich maneuver to remove an obstruction that's out of reach.)

3. Lay the dog on his right side on a flat surface.

4. Place both hands on the chest and press down sharply, releasing immediately. (If you do not hear air going in and out, switch to the mouth-to-nose method.)

5. Continue until the dog is breathing on his own, or as long as the heart is beating.

Mouth-to-Nose Method: Follow steps 1 and 2 above, then:

3. Pull the tongue forward and keep the lips closed with your hand.

4. Take a breath and, with your mouth over the dog's nose, blow a steady stream of air for three seconds.

5. Release to let the air out. Continue until the dog is breathing or as long as the heart is beating.

HEART MASSAGE

When heart massage is combined with mouth-to-nose resuscitation (it takes two people), you are performing canine CPR. Heart massage alone, however, also brings air to the lungs.

To perform, follow steps 1 and 2 above for chest compression, then for small dogs and puppies:

3. Standing in back of the dog, place one hand on the sternum (bottom of chest) behind the dog's elbow with your thumb on top, fingers beneath.

4. With the other hand above your thumb, over the heart, press the chest firmly six times. Count to five (to let the chest expand) and repeat until the heart is beating

or no heartbeat is felt for five minutes.

For large dogs, follow the same procedure but place the heel of your hand on the rib cage behind the elbow (which will be over the heart).

THE HEIMLICH MANEUVER

This is the method used to clear the dog's air passage when he's choking. He'll be breathing hard, coughing, pawing at his mouth and in a panic. Put one hand over his nose, pressing down on his lips with your thumb and forefinger. With your other hand, press down the lower jaw to pry his mouth open.

If you can't see anything or feel anything with a finger, lay the dog on his side and lower his head by putting a pillow under his hindquarters. On a puppy or small dog, place one hand a few inches below the bottom of his rib cage (the sternum) and the other hand on the dog's back for support. (On a larger dog, place both hands below the sternum.) Press sharply in and up. Press until the foreign object is dislodged. What you are doing is literally "knocking the air out of him" so that the object is expelled by the force of the air. Should the dog be

Applying abdominal thrusts can save a choking dog.

unconscious, perform artificial respiration and get on your way to the veterinarian.

Specific Injuries

BURNS—Burns are caused by many things, such as touching a hot surface, fire and even sunburn. Severe burn of any kind can proceed to shock and the prognosis is poor. Small superficial burns can be treated by soaking with cold water or ice packs for fifteen to twenty minutes just to relieve the pain. Then trim surrounding hair, wash with surgical soap and gently blot dry. Apply antibiotic ointment. If the area needs protection (for example, when the dog lies down or walks), wrap it loosely with gauze.

BLEEDING—Bleeding is one of the primary concerns for first aid. Bleeding of a minor wound can be stopped by first cleaning the area with antiseptic and applying a gauze

67

pad, then bandaging with even pressure using gauze or any clean available material. Watch for signs of swelling or discoloration below the bandage that indicates a loss of circulation, in which case loosen or remove the bandage immediately.

Arterial bleeding comes in bright red spurts and requires a thick pressure pad (as above) plus additional pressure applied by hand. A tourniquet can be applied to the tail or leg above the wound, between the wound and the heart, but it must be loosened every twenty-five to thirty minutes. Proper application of a tourniquet is essential and is best left to a professional.

BROKEN BONES—Broken bones may be made worse by handling. In puppies a common type of break is a "green-stick fracture," in which one side of the bone is broken, and the other is bent. A compound fracture (where the skin is pierced by the

broken bone) should first be covered with a clean cloth. Immobilize the area and transport the dog (preferably on a rigid surface) as carefully and quickly as possible to a veterinarian.

DOG FIGHTS—Dog fights are very dangerous for dogs and people. If two dogs cannot be pulled apart by means of their leashes, separating them is best left to a pair of strong men, who are likely to be bitten in the process no matter what means of separation they try. A harsh stream of cold water may work, but not often enough to recommend it. Throwing a coat or blanket over the two heads will often cause one of the dogs to let go for an instant— but in that instant, someone has to be ready to pull them apart by their tails or hindquarters. A shrill personal alarm (used to deter a hold-up) may distract the dogs and cause them to desist. Similarly, mace or mace-type spray may break up the fight. Avoid inflicting pain on either dog because it will only increase the dog's aggression. Avoid giving the appearance of siding with either dog. Clean all bite wounds thoroughly, especially small puncture wounds, and get the dog(s) to the veterinarian at once.

Make a temporary splint by wrapping the leg in firm casing, then bandaging it.

DROWNING—Dogs do not know how to swim naturally, and too often they get into the water, manage to swim a short distance and then are unable to get out. Pools are especially dangerous. Treatment is the same as for people. Get the dog onto land immediately, clean out his mouth, give mouth-to-nose resuscitation or even oxygen if available. Be prepared to treat for shock.

HYPOTHERMIA—Hypothermia occurs when a dog is exposed to extreme cold. For some dogs, just getting wet and moderately cold will cause the body temperature to drop dangerously. Bring the dog into a warm room. Wrap him in blankets, rub him with towels and place hot water bottles (containing warm water) under armpits, chest and stomach. When rectal temperature reaches 100°, feed honey or sugar and water.

HEATSTROKE—Immediate action is required should your dog suffer from heatstroke. The most common cause of this condition in dogs is from being left in a car. Even with the windows partially open and parked in the shade, on a moderately warm day it only takes minutes for the inside of a car to become a deathtrap. Dogs do not sweat, but pant to breathe in cool air. When the air becomes as warm as the dog's body temperature, this body-cooling system fails and the dog can suffer brain damage, go into a coma and die in rapid succession.

Speedy treatment is essential. Remove the dog to a cool place. Immerse him in a tub of cool water if possible, or wet him down with a garden hose or buckets of water. Wrap the dog in wet towels; add ice packs to the head, neck and groin area if possible and get to a veterinarian immediately.

POISONS—Because puppies are so curious, they are prone to getting into any number of potentially toxic substances. These include houseplants, outdoor plants, household substances like cleaning products, pesticides and medications and

Some of the many household substances harmful to your dog.

70

other chemical-based products like paint thinner, kerosene and so on. Specific plants to keep away from your dog are discussed in some detail in chapter 1. One of the most deadly substances is antifreeze, which tastes sweet to dogs. A few licks result in kidney damage. Only slightly more than that ends in death. Get veterinary help at once. There is no home treatment.

GIVING YOUR PUPPY MEDICINE

Some medicines are easy to administer, others are not. Some puppies will take pills or let you put ointment in their eyes easily, some will not. Ask your veterinarian for help and follow these instructions.

To put eye ointment in the eye without poking the puppy with the tube, stand behind your puppy and cuddle his head up against your legs. With one hand, gently pull the

Squeeze eye ointment into the lower lid.

lower eyelid away from the eye just slightly. At the same time, squeeze some of the ointment into the lower eyelid. When the puppy closes his eye, the medication will be distributed over the eye.

There are several ways to give your puppy a pill. The easiest way is to keep a jar of baby food on hand. Dip the pill in it and your pup should readily lick the pill (with baby food) right from your hand. For those that lick up the food and spit out the pill, you'll need to be more careful. Have your puppy sit and stand behind him, straddling his back. With the pill in one hand, pull your puppy's head up and back gently so his muzzle is pointing up. Open his mouth and very quickly drop the pill in the back of his throat. Close his mouth and massage his throat until he swallows. Before you let him go, open his mouth and check to see that the pill is gone. Follow up with a treat.

You can give liquid medication by pouring it into your puppy's mouth. Be careful that he doesn't inhale the medication instead of swallow it. An easier way is to measure the medicine into a chicken or turkey baster or a large eyedropper, put the tip of the baster into the puppy's mouth from the side (between the molars) and, holding the puppy's mouth shut, squeeze the medication in while you tilt his head backwards slightly so the medicine runs into (instead of out of) the mouth.

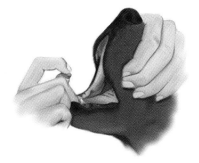

To give a pill, open the mouth wide, then drop it in the back of the throat.

Applying skin ointments is usually very easy—just part the hair so you're putting the ointment directly on the skin and rub it in according to directions. Keeping your puppy from licking the ointment off can be more difficult, and licking often makes matters worse. If your puppy has a bad skin condition or stitches that need to heal, your veterinarian will probably give you an Elizabethan collar for him. Named for the fashion styles of the reign of Queen Elizabeth I, this is a large plastic collar that extends at least to the tip of your puppy's nose. The collar is ugly and clumsy, and most puppies absolutely hate it, but it's the only way the wound will have a chance to heal.

Remember, whenever your veterinarian prescribes a treatment or medication, don't be afraid to ask questions. Find out what the drug(s) is, how it works and how long your puppy should take it. Ask if there are any side effects you should watch for. Make sure you understand what your puppy's problem is, what the course of treatment will do and what you should (or should not) expect. That done, make sure you follow through on the course of treatment. If your veterinarian said to give the medication for ten days, give it for ten days. Don't stop at five days just because your puppy looks better. Again, if you have any problems or reservations, call your veterinarian.

71

An Elizabethan collar keeps your dog from licking a fresh wound.

CHAPTER SEVEN

Pup Grows Up

As quickly as you can say, "My puppy never did (or never would do) that," you can be certain your puppy will! The fun of watching a puppy grow up is best reflected in the store of memories every puppy owner has of his or her pup's silly antics, the results of curiosity and faltering attempts at being a big dog. As your puppy grows up, she leaves you with this legacy of warm, smiling memories, many of which may be somewhat catastrophic and only amusing in retrospect.

If you ever owned a puppy before, or know someone who has, you don't need to be reminded that new puppies begin life with a canine version of "the terrible twos." Unsupervised, a growing puppy makes a demolition derby of everything in her path! The answer is simple—to prevent chaos, you must either supervise or confine.

Your care of the growing pup includes socializing her with other dogs and with people of all ages, preventing disaster, continuing education, remaining consistent in all you do and say, setting realistic goals, having great expectations and enjoying every minute of puppyhood that races by in a few months. A tall order? Yes, but together you and your smart, clever, wonderful puppy can do it!

THE BEST AGE TO BRING YOUR PUPPY HOME

While many trainers feel that precisely 7 weeks is the optimum age for puppies to go to their new homes in order to bond, more and more breeders are sending their pups out a bit later, between 8 and 12 weeks of age. This allows the youngsters to take advantage of learning firsthand from their mother and littermates what they need to know about being a dog. They learn to read body language, which is why your puppy watches everything you do or say and how you do or say it. They learn to respect a low warning growl or a sharp snap from Mom, which is why you can use that tone

of voice as a warning, or the imitation snap "aacht!" to get the same results.

MOUTHING

Puppies are worse than babies at thinking everything (whether or not it fits) is meant to go into the mouth. In addition, they also learn firsthand about licking. The dam licks her infant puppies to stimulate and to clean them—their first lesson in being groomed. Licking at their dam's mouth is both a submissive greeting and an appeal for food. Both domestic and wild female canids respond to lip-licking by regurgitating food for their young.

Some people like to be (what they call) kissed, but the majority do not appreciate all that licking! If you don't want your fully grown dog constantly licking at your hands and face, right now is the time to stop it. Create an unpleasant association by spraying a small amount of Bitter Apple on the back of your hand. As the pup approaches, offer the back of your hand and the pup will go away with a bad taste in her mouth. (Remember to wash it off or you may be the next unwary victim.) No need to scold or punish. Let her learn the lesson all by herself. And don't give up after two or three tries; it may take several weeks to curb the licking habit.

BITING

Another form of mouthing that is learned in the cradle, so to speak, is actual biting. Puppies mouth—and bite—each other in play. They may also experiment on their dam's ear or tail. What they get if they bite too hard is an "aacht!" combined with a hard and speedy bite back!

Puppies must learn to inhibit their tendency to bite. When your puppy tests her teeth on your hand, be quick to let her know that it is not acceptable. Scream, squeal or growl to let the pup know she hurt you, then stand up, move away and ignore her. "If you bite, I won't play" is understood by a puppy, especially one that had the opportunity to learn it from her littermates.

Another method is distraction. The pup is mouthing your hand and suddenly bites. Give her an "aacht!" and put a toy in her mouth, preferably a rope, towel or other chew toy she can get her teeth into (i.e., not a hard bone). It's not the time for chasing a ball. You want to make the

connection between what her mouth was doing and what it should be doing. It is difficult to keep all the things you need for teaching at your fingertips, but a small rope toy and a couple of treats will cover most situations.

A pup that has trouble learning to inhibit her bites may need to receive one sharp rap with two fingers on the top of the muzzle and a scowling, "No bite!" That's one rap with only two fingers—she's still a puppy, remember. It is the only time and the only form of physical punishment that is permissible. Then walk away and ignore her. This is not the puppy to play rough games with until she has learned to mind her mouth.

FEAR PERIODS

Each dog is an individual, and usually one fear period surfaces sometime around the age of 5 to 7 weeks. But don't be too surprised if your pup hits this stage at 10 weeks or never goes through it at all. The puppy that suddenly won't step off the familiar curb is not being stubborn or defiant or stupid. She is fearful. So instead of forcing her to step off the curb she suddenly finds terrifying by jerking or dragging her by the leash, use a cheery voice and an enticing treat. (You see? All puppy owners soon get used to having small treats in every pocket! And to always wearing clothes with pockets.) For other types of fear demonstrations, use distractions such as tossing a toy or calling the pup to chase you.

Responding to Your Puppy's Fears

It especially bothers puppy owners and their friends when the pup refuses to say hello. Yesterday you were teaching her not to bounce up on everyone, and today she's hiding behind your feet or under the bed! Pay no attention to this change. Ask friends to ignore her even when she is finally brave enough to crawl out to join the group, and also to remain still and silent, not to reach out to touch the pup or speak to her. Let the puppy sniff, and if she cozies up, that's fine, but don't be surprised if she darts away again. In a few days this skittish behavior will be history—that is, until the next fear phase.

    If you coddle the puppy during a fear period, she may get stuck in

that phase and forever be terrified of your guests, thunder, steps or whatever. A "fear phase" is a normal rite of passage for a puppy. It can occur again at around 5 months of age and once more between 10 and 15 months of age (before or after the teenage-adolescent stage). This is not the moment to introduce a pup to new people, places or things. If you recognize a fear phase, just play it cool for a week or so.

If your puppy is mouthing your hand and then decides to bite you, teach her the appropriate outlet for this action by giving her a toy to chew on instead.

A Dog's Senses

Sight: With their eyes located farther apart than ours, dogs can detect movement at a greater distance than we can, but they can't see as well up close. They can also see better in less light, but can't distinguish many colors.

Sound: Dogs have a much keener sense of hearing than we do, and they can hear high-pitched sounds especially well. Their ancestors, the wolves, howled to let other wolves know where they were; our dogs do the same, but they have a wider range of vocalizations, including barks, whimpers, moans and whines.

Smell: A dog's nose is her greatest sensory organ. Her sense of smell is so great that she can follow a trail that is weeks old, detect odors diluted to one-millionth the concentration we'd need to notice them and even sniff out a person underwater!

Taste: Dogs have fewer taste buds than we do, so they're likelier to try anything—and usually do, which is why it's especially important for their owners to monitor their food intake. Dogs are omnivores, which means they eat meat as well as vegetable matter like grasses and weeds.

Touch: Dogs are social animals and love to be petted, groomed and played with.

Trying to comfort a dog's fear only makes matters worse, because your words and tone of voice are misunderstood by the dog to be your approval of her being afraid! Noise fear is overcome with a little chit-chat, a distracting game or toy and a cheerful, unconcerned attitude on your part. Your puppy is taking in every minuscule part of your reactions. It's the old follow-the-leader ploy. If whatever it is doesn't frighten you, then the puppy will soon learn to trust your good judgment and follow your lead. Almost everything she learns from you is based on trust, so your primary goal is to be consistently trustworthy.

TEMPERAMENT DEVELOPMENT

At around 3 months of age, personality traits begin to emerge. You may suddenly notice that you have an affable bully, a playful clown, an incorrigible con artist, an adoring slave or a bashful sweetie. These are individual personality differences. Temperament problems at this tender age are seldom spotted by pet owners, which may be just one reason that they can become firmly established and increasingly difficult

Never doubt that your puppy knows how to get what she wants, even if this pursuit involves using her talents as a con artist.

to cure. If you have a problem that you can't solve, the quicker you seek professional help, the easier it will be to unravel.

GETTING AGGRESSIVE

Aggression may surface as fear-biting, where the pup dashes out from her crate (or behind her owner) to nip a person or other dog, and instantly retreat. This behavior is not related to the fear discussed previously. It is a form of aggression. Any form of real aggression—growling, snarling, snapping, biting—requires immediate professional help. It won't go away if you ignore it, and it can escalate quickly.

This is not the same as a pushy or dominant but good-natured pup that can be readily brought into line. The latter is a personality type many pet owners prefer.

It is vital that you end aggressive conduct now while she's still a puppy and, despite testing you in this way, she's still ready for you to be in charge. Aggression only feeds on aggression, so don't chase and do not punish the dog. Put her in her crate and leave her alone until she has calmed down.

SUBMISSIVE URINATION

Another behavior that will become an ongoing problem unless properly

come to you. By deliberately ignoring this type of puppy, the pup will develop a less submissive personality. Unfortunately, ignoring an adorable puppy is a formidable task.

MANAGING CURIOSITY

At the age of 3 months, your puppy's sense of curiosity will be at a peak, and for the majority of puppies, curiosity is kept in check by an equally natural sense of caution. This instinctual caution is self-preservation at work. The pup will slink like a cat toward her first encounter with anything from a fallen leaf to a silent vacuum cleaner. She has to meet each challenge in her own way in order to build self-confidence. It will go on to become a form of play. Don't interfere unless it's a life-threatening situation. Intense curiosity about a supposedly empty antifreeze container calls for immediate interference!

This is also prime time for mischief. You can expect toilet paper streamers (it doesn't only happen in TV commercials); underwear in the living room or a bath mat, towel or baseball mitt tucked at the back of the crate. Your puppy isn't being

If, when you reprimand your puppy for inappropriate behavior, your puppy responds with aggression, crate her and do not allow her to test you further.

handled is submissive urination, where the pup rolls over, exposes her vulnerable underbelly and wets. It occurs more frequently in bitches than in males, and is commonly found in certain breeds, such as Cocker Spaniels. This is not intentional urinating, but it is a dog's way of yielding to a superior authority. Therefore, it is never a punishable offense.

You can take steps to prevent activating undesirable submission. Avoid anything the pup can perceive as dominance, such as standing above her or reaching down a hand to pet her. Crouch to her level with your arms next to your body. Let her bad, she's having fun. Puppy fun. Re-examine storage of all medications, household cleaners, pesticides and everything you keep in the garage. Is your garden safe? Do you have any new (and possibly dangerous) household plants? If the puppy is around, don't put anything down for a second that could be harmful to her (or to the object) if she were to run off with it.

Even a contentedly confined pup, if she is not given enough exercise, may occasionally go stir-crazy and strip the wallpaper, remodel the kitchen cabinets or dig peepholes in a hollow wooden door. However, the pup that is not confined, one that has been "so good" (for all of two days!) that you have given her "freedom" of the house—that pup has been given the opportunity to trash your antiques, soil every rug or carpet you own, tear down the curtains and leave you wondering why in the world you ever wanted a puppy in the first place. Confinement is a kindness—to both of you.

TO SOOTHE TEETHING

At about 4 months of age, the puppy teeth fall out as permanent

YOUR PUPPY'S "HUMAN AGE" AND LONGEVITY

There are several ways of comparing dog years to human years, but the most widely-accepted method follows: The first dog year is the equivalent of 15 human years; the second dog year is the equivalent of 24 human years. Then add 4 years to the human's for every one of the dog's (3 equals 28, 4 equals 32, 5 equals 36, etc.).

As to longevity, a dog's size plays an important role. Broadly, small dogs live a long time (18 to 20 years is not uncommon) and giant breeds (Great Danes, Irish Wolfhounds) typically live only 5 to 10 years.

teeth erupt, and with them comes the most intense period of chewing. Rawhides and hard indestructible toys are only part of the solution. To soothe those sore, itchy gums, dampen and chill a knotted piece of toweling (an old hand towel is good) and give it to the teething pup as a toy. She'll enjoy the massaging effect of chewing into the terry cloth and the cold will help those itchy, possibly painful gums.

Don't try to play dentist; the teeth will fall out by themselves. You should, however, check the progress of tooth replacement when you

Curiosity is natural for all puppies, but some breeds, like Jack Russell Terriers, have especially strong investigative instincts.

brush the puppy's teeth. You should be looking for retention of baby teeth, with the permanent teeth erupting in front of or behind them. Obviously, keep an eye out for any development that does not appear normal.

All dogs chew (and bark, and wag their tails), but a teething puppy needs to chew. If you don't provide the right toys, the pup will satisfy her needs on chair and table legs, doors, rugs—you name it! The most dangerous of these undesirable objects are electric cords, especially those attached to toasters, coffeemakers and other light appliances, which take only one good yank to come crashing down. You

can't monitor your puppy every second, so smear or spray that cord with Bitter Apple—and for good measure, keep at least one eye on the pup.

PUPPIES AND CHILDREN

Puppies and children seem to be made for each other, but little kids need to learn the rules about their puppy. Let small children play on the floor or the ground with their puppy so they don't have to pick her up. However, because a small, soft, furry, cuddly pup is as irresistible to kids as to adults, it's a good idea to teach the kids how to pick up the puppy safely—safely for both the pup and the children.

Begin by having the children sit on the floor and scoop the puppy up into their laps with hands firmly (but gently!) around the pup's mid-section. No one should ever lift or pull a puppy or dog by the front legs. Dogs do not have the same shoulder rotation as people do and pulling on the front legs can do permanent damage.

Older children (and adults) pick up a puppy with both hands firmly, but gently, around the rib cage and slowly lift her to chest level, holding her firmly against the chest. Express elevator rides cause fright or nausea, so put the puppy down slowly, too, holding firmly until all four feet are on the ground before letting go. Puppies wiggle—sometimes frantically—and kids have to be taught the difference between "holding firmly" and squeezing!

It should be obvious that holding a puppy is not something that your toddler can manage. Toddlers drop or throw everything they pick up—including animals. Put the emphasis on patting the puppy gently and be ready to impose effective correction of the child for pinching or pulling the pup. Be especially wary when your puppy is eating and be sure to keep crawling babies and toddling toddlers away from the dog.

An older child should be encouraged to help with the pup's food and water, as well as grooming and training, all according to his or her ability in these areas. Don't expect to have all promises of caregiving fulfilled. Even if the kids aren't very adept at it, they will learn to think of others and something about the responsibility of owning a puppy.

A dog may bite a child for many reasons, but biting most frequently results from a child's teasing or

Teach your children how to hold your puppy properly before you let them pick her up off the ground.

81

Puppies can be great companions for children, but you'd be wise to supervise their play until your child is old enough to be aware of the dog's limits.

to taunt the dog. If you must, call for a time-out, both for the kids and for the puppy, who goes into her crate for a cool-down period.

Small children can hurt a puppy unintentionally (a toddler plops down on the sleeping pup, for example, or stumbles on a paw). As children like to test limits, they may even intentionally hurt the pup—let's see what happens when the ear is pulled, the eye poked, the leg bent backward. Kids need to be taught kindness to all living creatures, beginning with their puppy.

hurting the dog. Children are often not aware that they are teasing the dog. They wave their hands (with or without a toy or treat) over the pup's head to make the puppy jump up. The child thinks he or she is playing, but the pup sees it differently. To the puppy, it's a chase and she's trying to catch the object—which she does with her needle-sharp teeth, causing Molly to scream that she has been bitten. In reality, Molly has simply been "caught"—caught teasing the puppy!

A running child can be irresistible to a puppy, who will frequently go after the child's ankles. Children must learn that this behavior serves

FORMING GOOD HABITS

Young puppies should be kept off furniture for two long-term reasons. First, chairs, couches and beds are for people. Dogs have their own furnishings, which are kept on the floor. Second, and just as important, puppies are apt to make Superman leaps off furniture, which can permanently damage the growth plates in their legs, something that can't be seen until the deformity is visible months later.

For the same reason, don't try to force reluctant young pups to go down steps. Teach the puppy how to negotiate stairs when she is physically ready for it. If you want to see how scary going down stairs can be for a little puppy, go to the top of the steps and get down on all fours and have a good look. Now see how safe you'd feel about going down!

Puppies get away with doing things that are totally unacceptable in an adult dog. It may be cute to have your little puppy pouncing at your knees when you come home, but when she's a full-grown 140-pound Newfoundland, she'll knock you flat! Teach the young puppy right from the start the good manners you will want in your adult dog.

DEVELOPING YOUR PUPPY'S SOCIAL SKILLS

When the puppy's immunizations are effective, you can venture farther afield than your own backyard. Short walks and playtime in different environments are good for exercise and for socializing.

Playing on a beach or a stroll in the park will be full of learning experiences for a puppy. The retractable leash is perfect for these play-walks because it gives the puppy about 16 feet of controlled freedom.

A total of fifteen to twenty minutes is sufficient at first. You can add a few more minutes every few days depending on the pup (get home before she is tired), but also on the weather. Hazy, hot and humid days are not suitable for outdoor exercise. Icy pavements or streets may contain chemical melting agents, which must be washed off as soon as you get home. Take full advantage of time away from home to continue teaching your puppy. Commands such as "Come" and "Stay" as well as "Get it!" and "Give it!" can be practiced as part of a fun walk.

83

THE SIX-MONTH TRANSITION

This is a great stage of a puppy's life! Your pup has accepted most of your house rules. (All? She's a genius! None? What are you doing wrong?) She's big enough to go for longer walks and play more interactive games. The main issues to address are the possible return of a fear phase and the onset of sexual maturity.

At 5 or 6 months (but sometimes as late as 10 months), males will begin to lift a leg to urinate, and so begins the routine common to all

Socializing a puppy from a young age will help ensure that she learns to have positive interactions with people as she grows up.

male dogs of leaving a few drops of urine here, there and everywhere, often followed by kicking at the ground with the hind feet. This behavior is known as "marking territory." It serves a definite purpose in the wild, and is carried over in domestic dogs. It's the pup's way of saying, "I was here."

Clearly, this is not conduct that you want to occur in your home. Stop it with a sharp "aacht!" There is no need to punish the dog, because he is not urinating. It is natural male behavior that must be modified so it doesn't happen indoors whether you are home or not. Take that as a

warning: Marking can become an expression of a "separation anxiety" problem if you don't stop it. Clean up the drips with an enzyme cleaner (sold in pet stores) that will actually remove the odor, not just mask it. If you catch him more than twice at the same spot (refrigerators seem to get this preferential treatment), clean it up and then use a repellent. By 6 months of age, most dogs have reached about three-quarters of their full maturity. However, that refers only to their physical development. Mental maturity will take longer.

Neutering a male pup or spaying a female at about 6 months of age, or before sexual maturity, not only accomplishes the obvious (the prevention of unwanted pups), but has additional benefits, one of which is to virtually eliminate the incidence of cancers most often seen in the reproductive organs. In most towns a neutered dog earns you a discount—every year—on the dog's license.

At this age gardening becomes a favorite occupation for your puppy. The pup may watch you dig, cultivate or plant and says to herself, "I can do that!"—so she does. The companionship of a pup in the garden is not to be denied, so provide the pup with some of her own toys, and continue to teach her the boundaries of the garden beds. Choose a simple signal that suits you, such as "Out!" (pronounced "ow-wt" for emphasis).

THE TEENAGER

Doesn't that say it all? At almost any time between about 5 months and a year, adolescence strikes! Your adorable, cooperative, smart little puppy will eventually become a teenager and be her usual charming self one day, and a demanding, disobedient demon the next. You may find your previously placid pup stealing socks or food, or charging around the house like a wild beast with a tornado on her tail, then ending up panting by her water bowl with (you could swear) a smile on her face. Join the joke. These antics will soon be memories. Be your consistent, firm but good-natured self and you'll soon get through it. It may take more firmness, a few more time-outs and complete consistency, but remember to keep your cool. Puppy will be an adult for the rest of her life.

PLAYTIME

Playing is serious business for a dog. Your puppy doesn't stop learning because the two of you are playing with a ball. She is learning to get it and bring it back to you or, she soon discovers, the game ends. The development and reinforcement of trust occurs while playing. If you give the puppy a squeaky toy and suddenly hear silence, the pup has removed the squeaker and you have to remove the toy. One snatch attempt and you'll be nailed (it is her toy), so use "Give it!" with an irresistible treat in one hand. Remember your manners—say, "Good dog!"

Tug-of-war is a fun game that most puppies love to play, but this game may reinforce aggressive tendencies. Many experts advise that you avoid this game altogether.

Agility

Puppies like nothing better than their own playground. An old tire on its side is to climb in and out.

A carton open at both ends becomes a tunnel to run through or hide in. A huge beach ball or an indestructible Boomer Ball will make a soccer star out of any pup.

The Sandbox Set

Some people go so far as to include a sandbox (or sand pit) where the dog is meant to dig to her heart's content. *A cautionary note*: This is a great idea, but it can backfire. A dog that had never thought about digging will be taught how, and she may seek alternatives to the sand pit.

CHAPTER EIGHT

Recommended Reading

BOOKS

About Health Care

Ackerman, Lowell. *Guide to Skin and Haircoat Problems in Dogs.* Loveland, Col.: Alpine Publications, 1994.

Alderton, David. *The Dog Care Manual.* Hauppauge, N.Y.: Barron's Educational Series, Inc., 1986.

American Kennel Club. *American Kennel Club Dog Care and Training.* New York: Howell Book House, 1991.

Bamberger, Michelle, DVM. *Help! The Quick Guide to First Aid for Your Dog.* New York: Howell Book House, 1995.

Carlson, Delbert, DVM, and James Giffin, MD. *Dog Owner's Home Veterinary Handbook.* New York: Howell Book House, 1992.

DeBitetto, James, DVM, and Sarah Hodgson. *You & Your Puppy.* New York: Howell Book House, 1995.

Humphries, Jim, DVM. *Dr. Jim's Animal Clinic for Dogs.* New York: Howell Book House, 1994.

McGinnis, Terri. *The Well Dog Book.* New York: Random House, 1991.

Pitcairn, Richard and Susan. *Natural Health for Dogs.* Emmaus, Pa.: Rodale Press, 1982.

About Training

Ammen, Amy. *Training in No Time.* New York: Howell Book House, 1995.

Baer, Ted. *Communicating With Your Dog.* Hauppauge, N.Y.: Barron's Educational Series, Inc., 1989.

Benjamin, Carol Lea. *Dog Problems.* New York: Howell Book House, 1989.

—— *Dog Training for Kids.* New York: Howell Book House, 1988.

—— *Mother Knows Best.* New York: Howell Book House, 1985.

—— *Surviving Your Dog's Adolescence.* New York: Howell Book House, 1993.

Bohnenkamp, Gwen. *Manners for the Modern Dog.* San Francisco: Perfect Paws, 1990.

Dibra, Bashkim. *Dog Training by Bash.* New York: Dell, 1992.

Dunbar, Ian, PhD, MRCVS. *Dr. Dunbar's Good Little Dog Book.* James & Kenneth Publishers, 2140 Shattuck Ave. #2406, Berkeley, Calif. 94704. (510) 658-8588. Order from the publisher.

—— *How to Teach a New Dog Old Tricks.* James & Kenneth Publishers. Order from the publisher; see address above.

Evans, Job Michael. *People, Pooches and Problems.* New York: Howell Book House, 1991.

Kilcommons, Brian and Sarah Wilson. *Good Owners, Great Dogs.* New York: Warner Books, 1992.

McMains, Joel M. *Dog Logic—Companion Obedience.* New York: Howell Book House, 1992.

MAGAZINES

The AKC Gazette, The Official Journal for the Sport of Purebred Dogs. American Kennel Club, 51 Madison Ave., New York, NY 10010.

Bloodlines Journal. United Kennel Club, 100 E. Kilgore Rd., Kalamazoo, MI 49001-5598.

Dog Fancy. Fancy Publications, P.O. Box 6050, Missin Viejo, CA 92690.

Dog World. Maclean Hunter Publishing Corp., 29 N. Wacker Dr., Chicago, IL 60606.

CHAPTER NINE

Resources

BREED CLUBS

Every breed recognized by the American Kennel Club has a national (parent) club. National clubs are a great source of information on your breed. You can get the name of the secretary of the club by contacting:

THE AMERICAN KENNEL CLUB
51 Madison Avenue
New York, NY 10010
(212) 696-8200

There are also numerous all-breed, individual breed, obedience, hunting and other special-interest dog clubs across the country. The American Kennel Club can provide you with a geographical list of clubs to find ones in your area. Contact them at the above address.

TRAINERS

AMERICAN DOG TRAINERS'
NETWORK
161 West 4th Street
New York, NY 10014
(212) 727-7257

ASSOCIATION OF PET DOG
TRAINERS
P.O. Box 3734
Salinas, CA 93912
(408) 663-9257

NATIONAL ASSOCIATION OF DOG
OBEDIENCE INSTRUCTORS
2286 East Steel Road
St. Johns, MI 48879

ASSOCIATIONS

AMERICAN DOG OWNERS
ASSOCIATION
1654 Columbia Turnpike
Castleton, NY 12033
(Combats anti-dog legislation)

DELTA SOCIETY
P.O. Box 1080
Renton, WA 98057-1080
(Promotes the human/animal bond
through pet-assisted therapy and
other programs)

DOG WRITERS ASSOCIATION OF
AMERICA (DWAA)
Pat Santi, Secretary
173 Union Road
Coatesville, PA 19320

NATIONAL ASSOCIATION FOR
SEARCH AND RESCUE (NASAR)
P.O. Box 3709
Fairfax, VA 22038

THERAPY DOGS INTERNATIONAL
1536 Morris Place
Hillside, NJ 07205